# THE NEW GERMANS

# THE NEW GERMANS

GILES RADICE

MICHAEL JOSEPH

LONDON

*To the memory of Lilo Milchsack*

MICHAEL JOSEPH LTD

Published by the Penguin Group
27 Wrights Lane, London w8 5tz
Viking Penguin Inc., 375 Hudson Street, New York, New York 10014, USA
Penguin Books Australia Ltd, Ringwood, Victoria, Australia
Penguin Books Canada Ltd, 10 Alcorn Avenue, Toronto, Ontario, Canada m4v 3b2
Penguin Books (NZ) Ltd, 182–190 Wairau Road, Auckland 10, New Zealand

Penguin Books Ltd, Registered Offices: Harmondsworth, Middlesex, England

First published in Great Britain 1995
Copyright © Giles Radice 1995

Filmset by Datix International Limited, Bungay, Suffolk
Printed in England by Clays Ltd, St Ives plc
Set in 11.5/14.25pt Monophoto Bembo

A CIP catalogue record for this book is available from the British Library

ISBN 0 7181 3780 9

The moral right of the author has been asserted

# Contents

DENMARK

BALTIC SEA

NORTH SEA

Kiel •

SCHLESWIG-
HOLSTEIN

○ Rostock

MECKLENBURG –
WESTERN POMERANIA

Schwerin •

Hamburg

Elbe

Bremen ○

HOLLAND

LOWER SAXONY

Hanover •

Magdeburg •

BERLIN

Potsdam •

POLAND

BRANDENBURG

Rhine

NORTH-RHINE
WESTPHALIA

SAXONY-
ANHALT

Elbe

Düsseldorf •

Cologne ○

HESSE

Erfurt •

Leipzig ○

Dresden •

BONN

THURINGIA

SAXONY

BELGIUM

Wiesbaden •

Frankfurt ○

RHINELAND-

Mainz •

CZECHOSLOVAKIA

PALATINATE

SAARLAND

○ Nuremberg

Saarbrücken •

Stuttgart •

BAVARIA

Rhine

FRANCE

BADEN-
WÜRTTEMBERG

Munich •

AUSTRIA

SWITZERLAND

■ National and
administrative capitals

● *Land* capitals

○ Other major cities

–·–·– International boundary

·········· Former border between
East and West

– – – *Land* borders

0        150 km

(Map of Germany from *Germany and the Germans*
by John Ardagh, Penguin)

# Preface

What happens in Germany is vital to Britain and to the rest of Europe. This book, published fifty years after the end of the Second World War, is an assessment of the achievements and problems facing the Germans now. I have been fortunate enough to visit Germany regularly since the early 1970s and, in the last two years, have had the opportunity to interview well over 100 German politicians, civil servants, bankers, industrialists, trade unionists and academics in both West and East Germany. I would like to thank the Ebert *Stiftung* for their support in September 1993 and June 1994, the Deutsch-Englische Gesellschaft for arranging a lecture tour in February 1994 and the SPD for inviting me to observe the European and Federal election results at Party Headquarters. I am also grateful to German participants at successive Königswinter Conferences who have greatly assisted me in my preparation, as have my parliamentary colleagues on the Treasury and Civil Service Select Committee. The advice of the Warden and Fellows of St Antony's College, Oxford, especially Lord Dahrendorf, has been invaluable.

I would like to thank Penny Cooper, Professor Richard Evans, Klaus Funken, David Marsh and Lisanne Radice for commenting on drafts of the book, and thanks to Charles Handy for commenting on the Social Market chapter. Enno Berner, Penny Cooper and Sophie Radice have provided skilled research work. Enno Berner and Margaret Hansen have corrected my German spelling. My editors, Susan Watt and Alexander Stilwell, have improved the text. My thanks to the Goethe Institute and the House of Commons Library. I am especially grateful to Denyse Morrell for her patience in making sense of my

handwriting and for her excellent work on the word
processor. I take full responsibility for the views expressed
in this book.

Giles Radice
*February 1995*

## Introduction

## THE GERMANS AS THEY ARE

'Whoever closes his eyes to the past becomes blind to the present'

*Richard von Weizsäcker*

'The Germans appear to have found their self confidence in the strength and achievements of the democracy that was founded in 1949'

*Gordon A. Craig in* The Germans

At 2.41 a.m. on 7 May 1945, General Jodl, representative of the German High Command, and Admiral Dönitz, Hitler's successor, signed the instrument of unconditional surrender of all German land, sea and air forces at General Eisenhower's headquarters at Rheims. At one minute after midnight on 9 May all fighting was to cease. The war in Europe was over. Hitler, who had killed himself in his Berlin bunker on 30 April, had led the Germans to catastrophic defeat. Germany lay in ruins and was soon to be divided. As Winston Churchill, Britain's wartime leader, said in his victory broadcast on 8 May, 'Almost the whole world was combined against the evil-doers, who are now prostrate before us.'[1]

On 12 July 1994, Helmut Kohl, the Chancellor of a united, democratic and economically powerful Germany, walked with Bill Clinton, President of the United States, the world's only superpower, through the Brandenburg Gate, once a dividing line now the symbol of a united Germany. During his two-day visit, the American President had paid a glowing tribute to Germany's post-war achievements, to its special relationship with the United States, and to its leading role in Europe. '*Alles ist möglich*' (all is possible), declared Clinton, referring to the fact that, in under two generations, Germany had been transformed from pariah status at the *Stunde Null* (or Zero Hour) of 1945 to the very model of a modern European democratic state – '*Modell Deutschland*' as Helmut Schmidt, former West German Chancellor, called it – and was now being called upon to play a new role in Europe.

It has been a remarkable ascent, a 'rags to riches' story without parallel in European history. There have been a number of milestones on the way; the establishment of the Federal Republic in 1949, the end of Allied occupation and membership of NATO in 1955, founder membership of the European Economic Community in 1957, the signing of the Franco-German Treaty of Friendship in 1962, the Ostpolitik Treaties of 1970–72, founder membership of the European Monetary System in 1979, and, perhaps above all, the unification of the two Germanies in October 1990. The dramatic events which led to German unity, especially the fall of the Berlin Wall on 9 November 1989, caught the imagination of the whole world. An eloquent witness wrote of 'the magic, pentecostal quality ... Ordinary men and women find their voice and their courage ... These are moments when you feel that somewhere an angel has opened his wings.'[2]

But unification changed things. It changed the rich, comfortable, cautious Federal Republic into a different country – larger and more populous, but also poorer, arguably less stable and certainly more polarized. As the United States called upon it to play a greater role in world affairs, Germany found the process of uniting its two parts far more difficult than most politicians, especially Chancellor Kohl, had ever imagined.

Germany's European neighbours, who had grown used to an economically strong but politically flabby Federal Republic and who paid lip service to unification, became concerned about the implications of her bigger size. Margaret Thatcher, then Britain's Prime Minister, feared that a united Germany would be 'stronger than all the others', while François Mitterrand, President of France, was so worried that he flew to Kiev in December 1989 to discuss Germany's future with Mikhail Gorbachev, last President of the Soviet Union. Horst Teltschik, Kohl's security adviser, commented, 'Mistrust of the Germans runs deep.'[3]

A few years later, as German economic policy mistakes over unification had their impact, via high German interest rates, on other European economies and exchange rates, British and French ministers fumed at what they saw as German shortsightedness and insensitivity. After the humiliating departure of Britain from the Exchange Rate Mechanism in September 1992, the then Chancellor of the Exchequer, Norman Lamont, issued an angry press statement against the Bundesbank, while the Prime Minister, John Major, called in the German ambassador to protest. The ambivalence of British reaction was neatly summed up by a commentator in *The Independent*: 'Germany must not fail, thereby dragging the rest of Europe down, but it must not succeed to a degree that excites the envy of less fortunate countries such as ours.'[4]

In 1993, the editor of the British literary magazine *Granta* described the Germans as 'so ugly, so dangerous, so predictable'. A wild and offensive generalization such as this would have been understandable during or just after the Second World War, but, coming almost fifty years later in a serious journal, it reveals a profound ignorance of modern Germany. The sad truth is that, so long after the war and despite Germany being our main trading partner and fellow member of the European Union and the North Atlantic Alliance, the British know very little about modern

Germany. German is almost never the first foreign language taught in schools. Few learn subsequently about German politics, institutions or culture. Most British tourists go to France and the Mediterranean countries for their holidays. British views are shaped not by direct contact but an unhappy combination of national stereotyping, memories of two world wars (kept alive by TV soaps and the tabloid press) and half digested scraps of information. With a few notable exceptions (for example the *Financial Times*, *The Independent* and the *Guardian*), even the quality press provides inadequate coverage of Europe's most powerful nation.

The treatment of Germany and the Germans by the British tabloid press is a national disgrace. Over the Gulf War when Britain's European partners, especially Germany, were criticized for their inadequate contribution to the UN operation, the *Sun*, which announced 'We are so proud to be British', weighed in against Germany. After the headline 'MENACE OF THE GERMANS', it went on, 'At every turn, Germany has gone her own way. It has been *Deutschland über alles* – and everyone else can take a jump in the Rhine.' When it interviewed the German ambassador ('THE HUN MEETS THE SUN') it asked him, 'Why are the Germans behaving in such a cowardly manner during the Gulf crisis?'

Yet when, in an article in *Der Spiegel* in July 1994, the British Foreign Secretary, Douglas Hurd, welcomed the idea of German troops being used in a peacekeeping role, following the ruling of the Federal constitutional court that German forces could be deployed outside the NATO area, this was denounced by the *Daily Mail* under the astonishing headline 'ALL POWER TO THE GERMANS'. Totally inaccurately and ignoring the deep cuts in Germany's armed forces, the paper claimed that Hurd was supporting major German rearmament. It also quoted with approval Eurosceptic Conservative MP Nicholas Budgen as saying, 'I certainly don't want to see Germany's military power increase. It has provoked two world wars this century, and national characteristics don't change over such a short period of time.'

The announcement by the Prime Minister in March 1994 that Germany would participate in the VE-day commemorations on 7 May 1995 was greeted with press hysteria. Under the headline 'GERMAN ARMY TO MARCH THROUGH LONDON', the *Sun* said: 'Hitler's veterans will troop down Whitehall to Buckingham Palace – both prime targets during the Blitz . . . On the way they will pass the Cenotaph, where Britain remembers its war dead.' John Major pointed out that, while Germans would be invited to take part in the VE-day commemoration events, there was never any intention of allowing former Third Reich soldiers to march through London. 'I can assure you that no bemedalled veterans of the Axis powers will march or be wheeled past the Cenotaph during the events to mark the anniversary,' said a flustered Whitehall spokesman.

It could be argued that the tabloids and especially the *Sun*, should not be and are not taken too seriously. Yet these are Britain's most widely read newspapers and, at the very least, they make aggressive chauvinism respectable and legitimize the crudest kind of national stereotyping. Their underlying assumption seems to be that, despite the achievements of the Federal Republic, the Germans have not really changed and that, if the right opportunity presented itself, they would emerge in their true Nazi or Prussian colours. The verdict of British public opinion on the Germans is mixed. The British people took a far more relaxed view of German unification than Mrs Thatcher, believing that a united Germany presented no threat. They were also impressed by the way the Germans ran their economy and by their overall efficiency. Their main criticism at that time was that the Germans were arrogant and somewhat dull.[5] However, by 1994, according to a four-nation poll published in the *Guardian*, 50 per cent of the British distrusted the Germans (and 47 per cent of the Germans distrusted the British).[6] This is a disturbing finding which would seem to indicate that the combination of ambivalence by politicians, especially the Tories, chauvinism by the tabloids and perhaps also the problems arising from German unification, is now having an impact on British popular views. German attitudes are more a response to British prejudice and to anti-German campaigns in the British tabloids than a reflection of underlying distrust.

In a celebrated speech on the fortieth anniversary of the end of the war in Europe, Richard von Weizsäcker, then the highly respected President of the Federal Republic, told the present generation of Germans that their forefathers had 'bequeathed them a heavy legacy'.[7] It is certainly the case that Germany has a troubled past. At the beginning of the century, the Kaiser's expansionism and sabre-rattling diplomacy was a major factor in the outbreak of the First World War. Then in the 1930s the collapse of the Weimar Republic, Germany's first and unsuccessful democracy, was followed by the coming to power of Adolf Hitler and the Nazis with all that meant for Europe – the unprovoked attack on Poland in September 1939 which began the Second World War; the forty to fifty million combatants or civilians who were killed or died prematurely in that war; the deportation, torture and brutal treatment in prisons and camps; and the racist massacres, above all the deliberate extermination of nearly six million Jews. The sheer scale of the Jewish Holocaust, the horror of the death camps, the direct involvement of thousands of Germans, the cold-blooded planning and execution make it a crime apart. It was a German historian who wrote, 'Never before had a state . . . decided that a specific human group, including its aged, its women, its children and its infants, would be killed as quickly as possible and then carried through this regulation using every possible means of state power.'[8]

In the 1961 preface to his controversial *Course of German History*, the Oxford historian A.J.P. Taylor wrote that 'It was no more a mistake for the German people to end up with Hitler than it is an accident when a river flows into the sea.'[9] Those who share Taylor's view have tended to see German history as an inevitable process, a straight line starting with the relative weakness of the German enlightenment and the subsequent rise of nationalism, continuing with the failure of liberal democracy in 1848 in Germany as a whole, and then in the 1860s in Prussia, the 1871 unification imposed by force from above and the unstable and militaristic authoritarianism of William II, and culminating with the collapse of the Weimar Republic and the advent of Adolf Hitler. During the 1980s, an attempt was made by conservative historians, such as Michael Stürmer, historical adviser to Chancellor Kohl, to detach Hitler from the rest of German history by emphasizing Nazism's lack of roots, its dependence on the demonic genius of Hitler, and its similarity to Stalinism. The message was that the time had come to abandon guilt and give Germans a more positive view about their past. 'We cannot live by making our own past . . . into a permanent source of endless guilt feelings.'[10] This revisionism was denounced, in an article published in *Die Zeit* in 1986, by Jürgen Habermas, the distinguished philosopher from Frankfurt University who argued that it risked undermining the post-war commitment to pluralism and democracy and could even provide a rationale for a revival of Nazism and nationalist extremism. A fierce debate between these rival schools was fought out in the national media, the so-called 'Historiker-streit' (battle of the historians), without any agreed conclusion.

However, a way out has been suggested by the British historian Richard Evans in his fascinating account of the Historikerstreit.[11] He does not deny the continuities of German history nor that the roots of Nazism lie in the past. There were features in nineteenth and twentieth-century German society which, given a certain combination of events, led to Hitler. He does, however, argue that historical periods have to be seen not merely as a stepping stone to Hitler but in their own context. This seems a much more fruitful approach. It enables one, for example, to appreciate that Germany is one of the great cultural centres of Europe and that German achievements in architecture, music, literature and philosophy are among the landmarks of civilization.

The tourist in Germany can easily spot the traces of the Middle Ages – the great churches and cathedrals, the romantic castles on inaccessible crags (though some are later imitations), the splendid town halls (usually modernized during the Renaissance or in the nineteenth century) and, occasionally, even a breathtaking complete medieval city centre, as at Nuremberg, Regensburg and Rothenburg. If, under the complex arrangements known as the Holy Roman Empire of the German nation, the German lands developed on a far more fragmented and dispersed basis than England and France, German ideas, innovations and artistic accomplishments remained influential. Johannes Gutenberg, an illegitimate son of a Canon of Mainz, invented movable type in the fifteenth century, which revolutionized printing. In the sixteenth century Martin Luther's explosive religious ideas spread not only to the German-speaking world but to other countries as well, breaking the medieval unity of Europe into a mainly Protestant north and a Catholic south. In the late seventeenth and eighteenth centuries, following the Treaty of Westphalia which ended the highly destructive Thirty Years War, Germany of the *Kleinstaaterei* (or small states), became *das Land der Dichter und Denker* (the land of poets and thinkers).

Palaces and churches of real distinction were built in Germany during the eighteenth century. The marvellous Residenz which Balthasar Neumann built for the Bishops of Würzburg; the Zwinger, the joyous pleasure garden designed by Matthäus Daniel Pöppelmann for the Electors of Saxony at Dresden; the Catholic pilgrimage churches of Southern Bavaria and the rococo masterpiece, the Amalien-burg pavilion, designed by François de Cuvilliés for the wife of the Elector of Bavaria at Munich, are architectural achievements of the highest order. Even more impressive were the attainments of the sublime German composers of this period – Johann Sebastian Bach (1685–1750); Georg Friedrich Händel (1685–1759); Joseph Haydn (1732–1809); Wolfgang Amadeus Mozart (1756–91) and, at the end of this period, Ludwig van Beethoven (1770–1827). The latter three, Haydn, Mozart and Beethoven, looked to cosmopoli-tan and Catholic Habsburg Vienna for their inspiration and employment while Bach and Händel came from Protestant central Germany.

The German Enlightenment, the so-called *Aufklärung*, has received a mixed press. It started later and is generally considered to have been less pervasive and certainly more conservative than in France and Great Britain. The distin-guished American historian Gordon Craig refers to 'the relative failure in Germany of that great intellectual move-ment of the eighteenth century known as the Enlighten-ment.'[12] However, it threw up some towering figures, including the philosopher, Immanuel Kant, the poet, drama-tist and novelist Johann Wolfgang von Goethe and the playwright and poet Friedrich von Schiller, whose reputations spread well beyond Germany. The British historian of ideas Noel Annan believes that the 'German philosophers were perhaps even more influential than the Italian humanists had been in making men see the world through different eyes.'[13]

Turning to the nineteenth and twentieth centuries and Germany's failure to develop a responsible democracy, it is worth pointing out that other industrializing countries, including France, also had difficulties. There were features of Bismarckian and Wilhelmine Germany that showed considerable potential, including the role of the welfare state and a growing Social Democrat vote, while the Federal Republic has not only learned from the mistakes of Weimar but has also borrowed from some of its strong points. In other words, there is not a single echo from the German past but a number of echoes which remain of significance and value not only to Germans but to all Europeans.

This is not to disguise German disasters in the twentieth century or to brush under the carpet the evil regime of Adolf Hitler. Von Weizsäcker's advice to his fellow Germans remains valid:

> All of us whether guilty or not, whether old or young must accept the past. We are all affected by its consequences and held responsible for it . . . it is not a matter of overcoming the past. The past does not allow itself to be retrospectively altered or undone. But whoever closes his eyes to the past becomes blind to the present.

He concluded his commemorative speech with the ringing and challenging words:

> let us on the present 8th of May look truth in the eyes as well as we are able.

But if von Weizsäcker's advice is correct, it is no longer appropriate to judge today's Germans solely in terms of their past. After all, the majority of Germans were not even alive in the Hitler period. They have to be assessed against the background of what has been achieved since the war, and in the light of the problems which they are experiencing now and of their prospects for the future. This book considers the impact of unification on both east and west, and analyses the strengths and weaknesses of the Germans and their institutions. It also looks at the role which Germany is likely to play in Europe and the world and at its relations with other countries, including Britain. It is an attempt to describe the Germans as they are now, fifty years after the end of the Second World War.

Part One

# GERMANY UNITES

Chapter One

## ONE PEOPLE – TWO HISTORIES

Post unification joke –
*Ossi* to *Wessi*: 'We are one people'
*Wessi*: 'So are we'

The Berlin Wall was the symbol of divided Germany. Unification quickly followed its collapse. I first visited Berlin in summer 1962, a few months after the Wall had been erected by the East German regime, not so much to keep others out but to keep its own people in. With fellow British participants attending the first Anglo-German junior Königswinter Conference (including John Smith, future leader of the British Labour Party), I crossed into East Berlin at Checkpoint Charlie. After a brief discussion with our guide, the green uniformed East German frontier guards curtly waved us through. Being in East Berlin, even for a few hours, was a deeply depressing experience. Apart from a few pompous Stalinist official buildings, the rest of the city was crumbling and grey. You could almost smell the hopelessness and despair of the East Berliners who scuttled by with their heads bowed. We were relieved to get back to the bright lights and bustle of West Berlin.

After that unforgettable and saddening episode, I shared the delight of all Europeans as we watched on television the Wall being breached by East Berliners on the night of 9 November 1989. Three months later, I was appointed as an observer to a Congress of European Socialist Leaders meeting in the old Reichstag building in Berlin. In the lunch break, I and my Labour colleagues George Robertson, Mike Gapes and Larry Whitty were waved through the Brandenburg Gate, for so long the landmark of division, by the now friendly border guards. From the East Berlin side, we stopped and looked back through the Gate to the Tiergarten and the buildings of West Berlin and, on our return, we each bought a fragment of the Wall from an enterprising Berliner as a tangible memento of one of freedom's finest triumphs over oppression. It was a wonderful moment.

Most people had not expected unification until at least the next century. In 1987 the Soviet leader Mikhail Gorbachev told President von Weizsäcker that German unification might come in a hundred years. In January 1989, the leader of the GDR, Erich Honecker, proclaimed that the Wall would still be standing in fifty or a hundred years. West German leaders were cautious as well. In his memoirs, written in 1989, before the fall of the Wall, Willy Brandt, former SPD Chancellor and the architect of *Ostpolitik*, the policy of détente towards the East, remained sceptical about early progress. Even after the fall of the Wall, Helmut Kohl, the CDU Chancellor who presided over unification, continued for some weeks to assume that the other Germany would go on existing.

Why did the East German collapse come so unexpectedly and so quickly? After all, the GDR claimed to be the success story of the Eastern Bloc, a boast which was usually accepted at face value in the West. In 1988, the Encyclopaedia Britannica described it as 'The most developed and prosperous of the Communist countries and one of the major industrial nations of the world.'[1] Though there was emigration, especially of the most energetic and dynamic, there was little political unrest. While there were opposition movements in Czechoslovakia and in Hungary and, above all, in Poland, the quiescence of the East Germans was the butt of jokes throughout the Eastern Bloc.

The short answer is that it was external circumstances

which set off the epoch-making events in East Germany. A key role was played by Gorbachev. Now that he has been out of power for a few years, we begin to forget just what a profound impact the last Soviet leader had on the fate of the Eastern Bloc. At the June 1988 conference of the Communist Party, Gorbachev repudiated previous Soviet policy in Eastern Europe when he asserted the principle of freedom of choice and renounced the use of military force to prop up Eastern Bloc regimes. Gorbachev's new doctrine, described by his spokesman, Gennady Gerasimov, as the 'Sinatra doctrine' ('I did it my way'), acted as a green light for the Hungarians and Poles. In April 1989, the Hungarian Communists accepted the principle of a multi-party system, while in August, following partially free elections in Poland, the Catholic intellectual Tadeusz Mazowiecki became the first non-communist Prime Minister in Eastern Europe. Gorbachev urged Honecker to institute reforms in East Germany as well but Honecker and his elderly allies in the East German Politburo continued to resist. In October, Gorbachev personally gave the East German regime a decisive push over the edge. He used his visit to East Berlin to attend the celebrations of the fortieth anniversary of the East German regime in order to warn Honecker in a remark that was made public by his own press officer, 'When we fall behind, we are punished by life itself.' In the knowledge that Honecker no longer had the support of Moscow, Egon Krenz, Honecker's crown prince, and Günter Schabowski, party chief of East Berlin, plotted to remove him from power.

It has been said that German reunification should have been spelt 'Hungary'.[2] At the beginning of May 1989, the Hungarian Government started to dismantle its fortified border with Austria. In August, over 200,000 East Germans spent their holidays in Hungary and at least 25,000 of them took the opportunity to skip across the Austrian border en route to the Federal Republic. On 10 September, encouraged by the West Germans, Hungary opened its border completely and the stream of emigrants became a flood. Within three weeks, 40,000 went to West Germany through Hungary. Others sought exit routes via West German embassies in Prague and Warsaw. They simply drove to the embassies in their stinking Trabant cars and refused to leave until East Berlin gave them permission to go to the West. At the end of September, the GDR Government was forced to let the Prague squatters leave Czechoslovakia in a special train which travelled across East Germany to the Federal Republic. As the train passed by, people waved white handkerchiefs. When they crossed the border, the emigrants shouted, 'Freedom! Freedom!' It has been said that 'emigration is the German form of revolution'; and it is true that the sheer number of those leaving was a factor in the undermining of the East German regime. But by the autumn internal unrest had started to grow, with the Protestant Church providing a focus for dissent. In September, opposition groups, including New Forum, were formed, followed by growing public protests in Leipzig, Dresden, Halle, East Berlin and other cities.

The turning point was the massive demonstration of about 70,000 in Leipzig on 9 October – the biggest public gathering since the East German uprising of 1953. Since late summer, the regular Monday evening 'prayers for peace' in the Nikolaikirche had been followed by small demonstrations in the Karl-Marx-Platz (now renamed the Augustus Platz). As their size grew, so did retaliation from the security police. In early October, a demonstration was planned to press for democracy and the legalization of New Forum amid growing rumours of a Tiananmen Square-style crackdown. A huge presence of armed police, militia and Stasi gave credence to these rumours, as did tanks stationed around the city and hospitals preparing blood supplies and body bags. Despite the danger of a massacre, the Leipzigers bravely went ahead with the protest, chanting together, 'We are the people.' Afterwards a young woman told me how terrified she and her actor husband had been:

> The official newspapers had been full of threats. We could see the riot police and ambulances and had heard about the tanks around the city. Although I was very frightened, I went with my husband because we thought there was safety in numbers. We all felt that we had to walk together.

Miraculously, the expected violent reaction did not take place. The Stasi, police and armed forces simply melted away and the demonstration went off peacefully. A number of people have claimed credit for what happened or rather did not happen in Leipzig, including Krenz and Honecker. But there is no evidence that the East German Politbüro, apart from putting the security forces on full alert, gave any firm orders at all. 'Willing to wound, but afraid to strike, Honecker left the fate of the evening to the demonstrators themselves' is how a shrewd commentator summed up the attitudes of East German rulers.[3] Apart from those who crowded the streets of Leipzig, the real heroes were Kurt Masur, the director of the city's celebrated Gewandhaus Orchestra, Peter Zimmermann, a Lutheran pastor and Bernd-Lutz Lange, a cabaret star, who persuaded three local Communist Party secretaries to broadcast a joint plea for peaceful dialogue and non-violence on the afternoon of the 9th. It was this appeal which, in the absence of specific orders from Berlin, ensured that the demonstration was a peaceful one. Only when the course of events was clear was there a telephone call from Krenz authorizing a stand down of the security forces. Characteristically, Masur went back to the Gewandhaus to conduct a programme of Bach and Beethoven. Meanwhile in Berlin the Communist

conspirators, Krenz and Schabowski, speeded up their plans
to depose a now totally discredited Honecker. At the 17
October Politbüro meeting, the ultra orthodox Prime Minister, Willi Stoph, who had been recruited to their side,
proposed that Honecker stand down. One by one, the East
German leader's allies deserted him, so that in the end the
vote against him was unanimous. True to party traditions,
Honecker then raised his hand to vote for his own resignation and walked out of the room and power.

Egon Krenz, the grinning crown prince much derided
as a *Wendehals* (or wryneck bird) because of his opportun-
ism, became Party Secretary. That evening, he gave a
broadcast promising reforms and urging East Germans not
to emigrate. But events had already moved beyond his
control. Mass demonstrations continued. There were
500,000 protestors in Leipzig on 30 October and even
more in the first authorized demonstration on 4 November
in Berlin. The flood of emigrants increased, stimulated by
the reopening of the border to Czechoslovakia. On 7
November, the Government resigned and the following
day a new Politbüro was announced with Hans Modrow,
the relatively popular Dresden Party boss, as Prime
Minister.

On 9 November the unthinkable happened, almost by
mistake. The Berlin Wall was breached. The new East
German leadership had decided that the only way to
stabilize the deteriorating situation was to grant a general
right to travel, though they envisaged it happening in a
controlled, orderly way. Schabowski, now Party spokesman, announced the news that evening at the end of a
rambling press conference. At two minutes to seven, he
told reporters that the country's borders, including the
crossing points in Berlin, were to be opened and visas
issued to those wanting to travel. On being asked when

this was to come into effect, he shuffled his notes, failed to find the answer, and replied, 'From this moment.'

When this was announced on the evening television news, the effect was electric. East and West Berliners in their thousands rushed to the Wall. 'Open the Gate! Open the Gate!' they shouted at the Bornholmer Strasse crossing. At Checkpoint Charlie, the pressure of the crowds mounted. At about 10.30 p.m., the bewildered guards, acting without instructions, opened the gates at four crossing points in central Berlin. East Berliners streamed through to be greeted on the other side by embraces, singing, dancing and champagne. It rapidly turned into 'the greatest street party in the history of the world.'[4] Celebrations continued over the weekend with East Berliners pouring through the Wall, often in their Trabants, to look around and to spend their DM 100 official welcome money, issued by the West German Government, in the overflowing shops of West Berlin. Schabowski's elderly Russian mother-in-law, informed by her daughter that the border was now open, asked, 'Does that mean we will live in capitalism now?' On being told that it was indeed a possibility, she visibly brightened and said, 'Well, in that case, I think I'll hang about for a few more years and see what it's like.'[5]

Schabowski's mother-in-law did not have to wait that long. For if 9 November was the most joyful occasion in the GDR's history, it was also the beginning of its end. The prime movers in East Germany's *'sanfte Revolution'* (or gentle revolution), the pastors, environmentalists, peaceniks, revisionist Marxists, idealists and intellectuals, had wanted to reform East Germany from within, to create a separate democratic 'third way' between the Communist GDR and the capitalist Federal Republic. But the mass of the people, who were increasingly joining the demonstrations or voting with their feet by emigrating to West Germany,

wanted the higher living standards as much as the democratic freedoms of the Federal Republic. The quickest and
most certain way to obtain that desirable combination was
through unification – and 9 November had shown that
'people power' was now a strong enough force to achieve
it. After the breaching of the Wall, the slogans of the
crowds began to change from 'We are the people' to 'We
are *one* people'.

When on 19 December, after a meeting with Modrow,
Chancellor Kohl spoke in front of the Frauenkirche at
Dresden, his words were drowned out by shouts of 'Unity!',
'Germany, united Fatherland!' and 'Help us, Helmut!' It
was then, according to his later account, that he realized
the strength of popular feeling. Even after the breaching of
the Wall, his ten-point plan, announced on 28 November
in the Bundestag, had been a cautious document which
envisaged a leisurely path via 'confederal structures' to
unification. Following Dresden, however, he realized that
unification would have to come as quickly as possible.

The Modrow Government introduced spectacular political changes, including talks with the opposition, the promise of free elections, and the dismantlement of the Stasi.
But it was too late. As Kohl now understood, the GDR
was crumbling. In January 1990, it was revealed that it had
£12.9 billion foreign debts and that £72 billion would be
needed to clean up East Germany's energy industry. Strikes
and wage demands threatened industrial production. Meanwhile the opening of the Wall had not stopped the stream
of East Germans flowing westwards at a rate of between
1,000 and 2,000 a day. This mass haemorrhage not only
continued to undermine the GDR but also put pressure on
the Federal Republic. 'In the context of a disintegrating
GDR, and a West Germany threatened and burdened by
the strains of the opening of the Wall, there was clearly no

alternative to an equalization of living conditions and an integration of the economies of the two Germanies – and this inevitably implied political unification,'[6] was the shrewd summing up of the logic of Kohl's position by a leading historian. Ever the wily politician, Kohl almost certainly had another motive in the back of his mind. In the year of federal elections, espousal of unification would provide his faltering CDU/FDP coalition with a popular issue. And if it proceeded quickly enough and on West German terms, his new popularity in the East might provide an additional electoral bonus. It would certainly wrong-foot the main opposition party, the SPD, who, with the exception of their elder statesman, Willy Brandt, were cautious about a headlong rush to a unified Germany.

In retrospect, the key German election of 1990 was the one for the East German Volkskammer on 18 March – the first free vote in the East since the Communists took power in 1949. At first, opinion polls had predicted a victory for the newly formed Eastern SPD. However, Kohl took the initiative by organizing a new right-wing electoral alliance in the East, through which he was able to use the existing organization of the East German CDU, one of the former Communist 'stooge' parties, without being tainted by it. Kohl himself was the alliance's chief campaigner, arguing persuasively for speedy unification under Article 23 of the constitution. Under this article, the newly constituted Eastern Länder would simply apply to become part of Germany. Kohl's knockout punch was the promise of immediate monetary unification. His justification for what his SPD opponents saw as a blatant electoral bribe and Karl Otto Pöhl, then President of the Bundesbank, as economically risky was that, without monetary union at an advantageous rate for the East, emigration to the West would continue at the same ruinous pace. Yielding to the demand of East German demonstrators, Kohl

declared, 'If the DM doesn't come to Leipzig, then Leipzigers will come to the DM.'[7]

Kohl's currency decision was a great political success.
His right-wing Alliance won over 48 per cent of the vote,
while the early favourites, the SPD, got only 22 per cent,
with the reformed Communists further behind on 16 per
cent. The parties representing those who had started the
revolution, 'the Alliance 90', received a derisory 3 per cent
between them. The East Germans had voted decisively for
immediate unification with the Federal Republic. Fortified
by his electoral triumph in the East, Kohl vigorously and
skilfully pressed on with a twin track strategy – endorsement of unification by the four victor powers of 1945 and
speedy unification under his leadership. In February, he
and Foreign Minister Genscher had already persuaded the
Americans and the Russians to agree to a '2 + 4' formula
(the two Germanies plus the United States, the Soviet
Union, Britain and France) as the body to authorize the
external aspects of unification. Taking full advantage of
what he described as 'a window of opportunity', Kohl,
with the support of President Bush and Secretary Baker,
dealt directly with Gorbachev. The crucial meeting was in
July when Kohl and Gorbachev concluded a bilateral deal
in the Caucasus by which the Soviet Union recognized the
full sovereignty of a united Germany, including the freedom to join whichever bloc it wanted – which, in practice,
meant NATO. In return, Kohl pledged a ceiling of 370,000
troops for the joint German army as well as German
financial credits and subsidies for the Soviet Union. The '2
+ 4' Treaty, which formally opened the way for German
unification, was signed in Moscow on 12 September. It
defined the borders of Germany, including the recognition
of its Oder-Neisse border with Poland; it reaffirmed Germany's commitment to peace, including the renunciation
of nuclear, chemical and biological weapons; confirmed

the phased withdrawal of Soviet troops from German soil; and, above all, it ended the rights and responsibilities of the wartime allies in Germany and so gave the united Germany full and unrestricted sovereignty. Unimaginable a year before, the treaty was a triumph for Kohl and his Foreign Minister, Hans-Dietrich Genscher.

On 3 October, following economic and monetary union on 1 July, the two Germanies united. As midnight struck, a giant German flag was unfurled outside the Reichstag, the West German national anthem rang out, and President von Weizsäcker and Chancellor Kohl attended a huge party at the Brandenburg Gate. In December, at the first all-German elections, Kohl reaped his political reward when the CDU/FDP coalition was returned to power. It was at least in part deserved. For, more than any other German politician, Kohl had understood that there was no alternative to unification and, with great agility and skill, he had prepared the way for it.

Yet if Helmut Kohl derived the main political credit from what happened, this was not a unification imposed, like that of 1871, from above or by what the architect of that unification, Otto von Bismarck, called 'blood and iron'. It was a peaceful unification instigated by East Germans eager for the benefits which unity with the Federal Republic would bring. In this sense, the '*sanfte*' revolution of 1989–90, because it set off unification from below, completed the business left unfinished by the failed German revolution of 1848, whose leaders called for a united *and* democratic Germany. However, although '*die Wende*' as it was called, came from below, it was a lopsided unification demanded and, to a considerable extent, made by the East and not by the West Germans. As the constitutional form which it took showed, it was very much a case of the East joining the West.

The Eastern part brought with it a very different experience from its Western neighbour, a divergence which was bound to influence the new unified Germany. When Willy Brandt, as senior member, opened the newly elected Bundestag in the old Reichstag building in Berlin in December 1991 he warned: 'Walls in people's heads are sometimes more durable than walls made of concrete blocks.'[8]

Timothy Garton Ash graphically described the division of Germany this way:

> If you happened to live at the bottom end of the Friedrichstrasse in Central Berlin, you got liberal democracy, the Americans, the European Community, the Costa del Sol, the Volkswagen and McDonald's. Your mother, who lived three blocks up the street, got Communism, the Russians, Comecon, the Black Sea, the Trabant and Soljanka.[9]

The West Germans had received by far the better of the post-war deal. They had the advantages both of a democratic society and of a social market economy. Politically they benefited from a system of legal rights, pluralistic choice and decentralized power. Economically and socially, they enjoyed high and rising standards of living, generous welfare benefits, decent housing and education, and the freedom to travel throughout Europe and beyond. By contrast, the East Germans lived in the most rigidly orthodox communist state in the Eastern Bloc. The state bureaucracy, local government, industry, the trade unions and the media were all firmly under the control of the party. The state security – the Stasi – was pervasive. It employed 85,000 full-time staff and a further 500,000 paid informers, supplemented by 1 million informal agents.[10] The Stasi ran a system of what its chief spymaster, Markus Wolf, called 'total domestic surveillance', keeping files on over a third of East Germany's sixteen million inhabitants. Little wonder that its critics called the GDR the 'peep and snoop' society.

Helped by West German subsidies, Honecker, who came to power in 1971, bought the acquiescence of East Germans with living standards which, though they were far lower than those of West Germany, were at least superior to other Eastern Bloc countries. But there were obvious 'blackspots'– poor housing, growing neglect of the infrastructure and environmental disaster areas. West German TV was available in most parts of East Germany, so people could see what they were missing. It is indeed legitimate to ask why the 1989–90 revolution, or at least the emergence of opposition on the scale of Solidarity in Poland, did not happen sooner. Part of the answer is that the regime had significant if minority backing. The 16 per cent vote for the PDS in the first free East German elections is some indication of the population supporting the GDR. I remember being struck by the fierce ideological commitment of a former radio journalist to whom I talked at a British embassy party in East Berlin in July 1990. 'My life's work is about to go down the drain,' he remarked bitterly. There were many more who, like the officious night security man in my East Berlin hotel, owed their employment to the party or who, like the genial official who showed us round Rostock harbour in 1993, had to become party members to rise in their professions. 'It went with the job' was a frequent comment. There was also, it has to be said, a strong streak of obedience to authority, engendered by a combination of fear of the Stasi and sheer social conformity. Nearly sixty years of totalitarian government, beginning with Hitler in 1933, had left its mark on East Germany.

In contrast to other Eastern Bloc countries, those who were outright opponents usually had the option of emigrating to the West. Asked in July 1989 what they considered to be the main reason for the weakness of the opposition in the GDR, compared with Poland, Hungary and Czechoslovakia, a group of dissident activists in East Berlin unanimously gave emigration as their first answer.[11] Getting rid of political opposition leaders, sometimes in exchange for West German currency, was an important safety valve for the regime. It also helped demoralize those who were left behind. The jibe that the initials of the DDR stood for '*Der doofe Rest*' (the dopey dregs) had just enough truth in it to hurt.

I asked a former Halle research scientist, who is now working for the Sachsen-Anhalt Land government, why he had not left East Germany. 'I stayed because of my roots in Halle and in the church. I also felt that I had to work towards a civil society with a functioning set of civil values,' was his reply. Meanwhile, he and his professional class friends sought compensation in a full private life, discussing books, throwing small dinner parties, going to art galleries, concerts and the theatre, and hiking in the countryside. The GDR has been called a 'niche society', in which, provided one kept out of politics and did not make trouble for the regime, one could do what one liked in one's private life. Yet many intellectuals paid a high psychological price for their 'inner emigration'. As an engineer member in Schwerin told me, 'For thirty years, I have suffered from being a thinking person in a police state.'

Until 1989, the East Germans had acquiesced in a political situation which they felt that they could not personally change. In return, they got cheap food, free medical care and education, inexpensive holidays (if only in Eastern Europe) and, by Eastern Bloc standards, a relatively good supply of consumer goods, supplemented by gifts from the West. It was only when they realized that the regime was in a state of collapse that they demanded for the whole of East Germany what only a small minority had sought before – full access to the political rights and economic prosperity of West Germany.

Lothar de Maizière, the GDR's only democratically elected Prime Minister, hoped that the East would be able to bring something of its own to unification. Yet the virtual collapse of the GDR, the lack of strong internal leadership and the desire of most East Germans to unite as quickly as possible meant that unification was a virtual Western takeover of the East. It was inevitable, however, that the method and speed of unification, combined with the very different recent histories of the two parts, would lead to tension and mistrust. As a German journalist wrote,

> The prognosis for the day the Wall came tumbling down was that Germans would discover they differed more than they agreed. After forty years of living under such unequal conditions, it seemed likely that they would feel things other than tenderness for one another: lack of understanding, prejudice, envy, even hatred . . . For it was the Wall alone that preserved the illusion that the Wall was the only thing separating the Germans.[12]

## Chapter Two

## TAKEOVER IN THE EAST – COLONIAL BACKLASH

*'There will be blooming landscapes within three years'*
*– Helmut Kohl at the Frauenkirche, Dresden in 1990*

These words, so full of promise, returned to haunt Helmut Kohl. The euphoria of 1990 proved to be misplaced. The German Government grossly underestimated the difficulties of amalgamating two peoples who had gone through such different political and social experiences and which were at such different stages of economic development. In addition, a number of policy errors were made, especially monetary union at a one to one rate. As a consequence of these errors, as well as the virtual collapse of Eastern European markets, a surge in East German wage rates and ruthless competition from West German firms, East German industry, which was, in any case, very uncompetitive on world markets, has been largely destroyed. The result has been a dramatic increase in unemployment in the Eastern Länder, real social discontent, considerable resentment of what the *Ossis* see as a West German takeover and even, in the phrase used to me by Hans-Jochen Vogel, former leader of the SPD and ex-mayor of Berlin, 'nostalgia for the GDR'.

I am fortunate enough to have been able to see at first hand something of the remarkable transformation which East Germany has been undergoing. In the summer of 1990, during the interregnum period between the collapse of the Communist regime and unification when the GDR had its first and last democratic government, I visited East Berlin as a member of the House of Commons Treasury

Select Committee, which was collecting evidence on the impact of unification on European monetary developments. It was a curious half world. Many of the old Communists were still in place at the State Bank, in the bureaucracy and in the universities. But they understood very clearly that their time was up. 'Who wants to know about Marxist economics now?' an economics professor sadly asked us.

There were also the idealistic leaders of the *sanfte Revolution* – the pastors, pacifists and intellectuals. I went to see them busily legislating themselves out of existence in the Volkskammer, the former GDR parliament which had been changed into a democratic assembly by the March 1990 elections. My friend, a German pastor who had become a temporary SPD MP, remarked wryly when I visited him later in his comfortable house in the suburbs, 'Our time never really came at all – or, if it did, it only lasted for a few months.' But, despite his regrets, he remained a strong supporter of unification which he saw as the only realistic answer. His daughter, who was excitedly packing for her first trip to the United States, was ecstatic. 'You in the West do not understand what a marvellous gift the freedom to travel is.' But perhaps the most potent symbol of the changes which were sweeping over the GDR was the line upon line of East Berliners eagerly queuing to register their savings at East German banks, so that they could qualify for the 1 to 1 exchange rate for the first 4,000 Ostmarks into D-Marks (otherwise it was to be at a 2 to 1 rate), for the arrival of our parliamentary delegation had coincided with the run-up to the currency union with West Germany. East German shops were empty in preparation for the flood of West German goods which would become available on 'D-Mark day' on 1 July. The D-Mark was about to become king.

In Frankfurt a day earlier, we had asked Karl Otto Pöhl, President of the Bundesbank, about the implications of the

1 to 1 monetary union of the two Germanies. He had admitted to us that he had warned Chancellor Kohl of the dangers to East German industry of too high an exchange rate. Others, particularly the economists at the Deutsche Bank, were more sanguine. But, as we watched those Berlin queues, we reflected and later reported to the House of Commons about the possible consequences, especially on East German output and employment, of such a generous rate of exchange. To that extent, we predicted some of the dangers ahead.

A few months later, in the spring of 1991, I was invited to the annual Anglo-German Königswinter Conference which was being held in Dresden on the Elbe in recognition of the importance of German unification. Despite the formal agenda, the subject of unification inevitably dominated the conference. I learnt from my German friends about the collapse of East German industry, the rising tide of unemployment in the East and the growing division between *'Ossis'* and *'Wessis'*. There was a new term, *'Besser Wessi'*, for the 'know-all' West Germans who were arriving by the planeload to teach the East German 'colonials' how to do it.

Already at Dresden Airport there was a feeling of coming to a 'colony'. Prosperous West Germans walked confidently to their smart Mercedes, parked next to clapped out East German Trabants. In the foyer of our grand conference hotel, shoals of West German businessmen swarmed, whilst at a conference reception a young *Wessi* market research 'whiz kid' told me that East German managers knew nothing about modern management techniques. Kurt Biedenkopf, the newly elected Land Prime Minister, himself a CDU politician from the West, explained to us the problems facing East Germany. Indeed these were only too obvious. Dresden looked terribly run down and shabby. To their lasting shame, the GDR authorities had failed to reconstruct fully the baroque centre, the glory of the old

Saxon capital which was brutally destroyed by the Allies in February 1945. We could also see black stains on existing buildings caused by old-fashioned polluted factories and the indiscriminate use of brown coal. A Dresdener who had been a teacher of Russian but was now a tourist guide told me that unemployment was climbing inexorably and that life was very difficult. 'In 1989, I was one of the demonstrators against the old regime. Now I am demonstrating against unemployment.' Clearly the heady optimism of the early days was rapidly disappearing.

Two-and-a-half years later, in September 1993, in company with three well-known British journalists and the London representative of the Ebert *Stiftung*, the SPD think-tank, I travelled the length of the former GDR, visiting four out of the six new Länder. We saw little outward sign of poverty or need. The shops were full, there were many new service industries springing up and there was a most striking and impressive investment in basic infrastructure projects. But it quickly became apparent to us that the overriding fact about the new Eastern Länder was 'de-industrialization'. There had been a massive destruction of jobs since unification. Employment in manufacturing had fallen to under 700,000, down 66 per cent from the two million it had been at the beginning of 1991. Taking into account the various employment and make-work schemes, the effective rate of unemployment overall was now over a third of the labour force.

After landing at Hamburg airport, we entered the new Land of Mecklenburg-Vorpommern by crossing the old GDR border near Gadebusch in Schleswig-Holstein. We quickly spotted the differences with West Germany, but there were also surprising similarities. We noticed the huge fields (partly because of collectivization), the decrepit rural housing as well as the occasional incongruous-looking

block of worker flats attached to villages. But we also
saw the shiny West German models on the resurfaced
roads, the car showrooms, new petrol stations, supermar-
kets, garden centres and DIY markets by the roadside.
There are other signs of a burgeoning consumer society –
house repairs and modernization going on, as well as
satellite discs sprouting up like ugly toadstools in every
village. And the road signs, telephone boxes and bus stops
were now West German. Our comfortable hotel at
Warnemünde, a faded resort by the Baltic, was newly
modernized and there were a number of trendy and expensive clothes shops beside the harbour. And there were no
problem in ringing London direct, so it was clear that a
spanking new telephone system was now being installed
in the GDR.

The following day we cruised up river past the shipyards,
many of them idle, to Rostock, to be briefed on the old
Baltic city's problems in the fifteenth-century Rathaus.
Rostock, which was the GDR's main port and shipbuilding centre, was faced by a drastic rundown of all its
existing activities. Under the GDR, the port handled all
incoming traffic and goods. Now it is no longer a major
terminal port, its shipbuilding has lost its markets, whilst its
textile industry has virtually ceased to exist. The SPD city
councillor responsible for Rostock's economy, Senator
Heinz Werner, a bearded *Ossi* in his forties, did not try to
hide the gravity of the situation. 'We have an unemployment level of at least 40 per cent, with all that means in
social problems,' he told us. Flanked by a CDU councillor
in charge of finance (Rostock was governed by a grand
coalition), he explained to us the city's bold recovery
strategy – expanding ferry services to the Baltic, developing
the port as a road and rail head to and from Berlin and as a
centre for the import of building materials and export of
grain, creating an innovation and technology centre at the

university, and setting up small and medium-sized businesses.

We discussed the social impact of all this change with a wider group of city officials and shop stewards. The general conclusion was that people in the East were now more pessismistic – there is high unemployment amongst young people, the older people feel pushed aside, and there is a big growth in crime. A *Wessi* official, Herr Backes, who was in charge of the employment office started an interesting *Ossi-Wessi* debate by saying that *Ossis* still feel second class citizens. According to a Rostock poll, over 60 per cent think that East Germany is a 'colony'. Another *Wessi* adviser said that democracy presented problems – in the East, there is no 'culture of debate'. He was immediately contradicted by an *Ossi* shop steward, who maintained that there was now more debate in the new Länder than in the old ones, though he undermined his own point by saying that 'the biggest grudge against the Communists is that they stopped people thinking.' He maintained that, even though people were disappointed by the lack of progress, there was still an underlying feeling of optimism, but there must be a more solid economic base.

Neubrandenburg, where we arrived the next day, has medieval fortifications and four magnificent gates but, under the GDR, became an industrial centre with construction works, pharmaceuticals and the largest tank repair factory in the Warsaw Pact. We were met by Joachim Willhoefft, a young SPD member of the Mecklenburg-Vorpommern Landtag, and conducted to an impressive new technology centre at the entrance to the tank repair factory. The general manager, Herr Noack, a former technical officer in the East German army, told us that all the big enterprises in Neubrandenburg had collapsed, except an oil heater manufacturer. Officially only 19 per cent were

unemployed but, taking account of job creation and training schemes, the real figure was nearer 40 per cent. The
role of the technology centre, paid for by the Land and the
town, was to stimulate small and medium-sized firms,
which it was hoped would eventually take the place of the
old industries.

The tank repair factory, RWN, which used to employ
4,000, now had only 200 workers. The old style manager
of the factory, Herr Schenk, had been given the task by the
Treuhand (the East German privatization agency) of breaking up the works into smaller companies. His only consola-
tion was that, despite the difficulties of working with the
Treuhand, he was at least selling the firms to East
Germans.

If Herr Schenk was authentic GDR, Heinz Schewe, a
former employee of RWN, now owner and manager of a
RWN successor company making aluminium frames and
windows, was very much the prototype of the new Eastern
Germany. Burly, fast talking and wearing a white wind-
cheater, Herr Schewe told us, 'I worked myself up the
ladder in the tank factory and then Erich Honecker disap-
peared. So what was I to do?' What he did was to take to
capitalism like a duck to water. After surveying the market,
he and a partner bought out one of the RWN subsidiaries
with a bank loan. Now he employs eighty people, has a
turnover of DM 15 million and a full order book. 'Every
mark goes back into the firm,' he assured us proudly.

At lunchtime, we were taken to the site of Pharma, a
vast penicillin factory which came on stream just six
months before unification. Dr Manfred Pfeifer, a balding
scholarly chemist and the company's former research director, explained to us what happened next. 'Our enterprise
had absolutely no contact with the market. We produced
to a good standard but regardless of cost. We looked for a
Western purchaser but were soon forced into liquidation.'

Pointing to the shell of the old factory, Dr Pfeifer wryly said, 'The empty building is a monument to the GDR.' He was now working for the Bremen-based liquidator and there were already a variety of small companies established on the site, mostly service based. The company's hostel had become a cut-price hotel, run by Dr Pfeifer, with a so-called 'English bar', much frequented by *Wessis* working in the Neubrandenburg area.

In the afternoon, we drove out to a village nearby, called Puchnow. Though formerly the centre of a large collective farm, Puchnow had an old-world feel to it – a street of single-storey houses with gardens and pink and red holly-hocks, a village green, and a Junker manor house built just before the First World War. We were shown around by the deputy mayor, Herr Skultety, who introduced us to a new phenomenon – a former co-operative member, Dieter Sünboldt, a bearlike man in a leather jacket, who had been suddenly transformed into a large-scale farmer. He was closely interviewed by the *Financial Times* correspondent, Ian Davidson. Apparently in 1991, the 360 members of the local co-operative received vouchers valuing their shares. In exchange for an undertaking to pay off the other members over five years, Sünboldt and a partner now farmed about 7,000 acres, on which they paid DM 300,000 rent, and employed thirty-one members of the former co-operative. What had happened to the other 329 members? It was difficult to get a straight answer, though it became obvious why in Mecklenburg-Vorpommern the number of farm jobs had dropped from 180,000 to 25,000. We were also told that there was a continuing muddle over land tenure. For example, the efforts of the original owners to acquire the family land had been rejected in the courts, but Herr Sünboldt thought that they would get back the manor and surrounding buildings.

The question of property ownership was still a major issue in the new Länder. Those whose property was confiscated under Hitler or under the Communist regime could make claims through the courts or local authorities to establish ownership or compensation rights. There had been a flood of Western claims, which had not only held up decisions about investment but had also led to considerable *Ossi* resentment. In Potsdam, which is not only the site of Frederick the Great's wonderful rococo pavilion retreat but also a very attractive lakeside resort, we were told that 80 per cent of property claims had not yet been cleared up. In Dresden, which used to be called the 'Florence on the Elbe', at least 40,000 claims were outstanding. 'Why should these rich *Wessis* who have not had to put up with the hardships which we have experienced now come and deprive us of our houses?' was one *Ossi* comment.

But, alongside the collapse of old industries and disputes about property, here and there we saw the green shoots of new investment. In Leipzig, a trade and cultural centre for centuries, the city of Johann Sebastian Bach, Felix Mendelssohn and August Bebel, founder of the SPD, we visited the McCain-Brehmer works, a brand new plant making machinery for bookbinding. In 1991, a big GDR state organization was bought up by McCain, a Chicago firm, which proceeded to close its old plants, sell off most of the sites and build a new plant. The work force had been reduced from 2,800 to 480 employees. The result was an enormous leap in productivity and, hopefully, viable employment for those workers who were left. We asked Gunther Boldin, a former GDR trade unionist now repackaged as the elected head of the Works Council, to compare the situation now with the old regime. He was very concerned about unemployment but he also added, 'Then you had money with nothing to spend it on. Now most have some money. The key difference is that there is so much more to spend it on. The timid may prefer the old certainties, the courageous may see the opportunities.'

In Dresden, the spokesman of the Biedenkopf Land government, Michael Sagurna, a smooth and sharp suited journalist from West Berlin, was optimistic. He admitted that the traditional industries, such as machine tools, textiles and lignite mining, had mostly collapsed and that Saxony, in the 1930s the strongest manufacturing region in Europe, faced de-industrialization on a massive scale. Building on a long tradition of precision instruments the Land government's strategy was 'to provide a home for high tech industry.' Their advantages include a highly skilled labour force, top class universities, a big expansion in construction, graphically demonstrated by the number of cranes in Dresden and Leipzig, and a growing service sector. The glossy *Investing in Saxony* brochure which he gave us emphasized 'the largest infrastructure programme in Europe', an ultra-modern communications system, and a spanking new road and rail network. This approach was already paying off. Volkswagen had built a new plant near Zwickau and Siemens were planning to make computer chips in the Dresden area. The spokesman stressed Saxony's favourable geographical position in the centre of Europe, 'balancing between East and West', and talked persuasively of the possibility of joint enterprises with the Poles and the Czechs, combining German 'know-how' and quality design with the lower costs of their eastern neighbours.

There was an impressive process of reconstruction going on in the historic centre of Dresden. We were told by the city councillor in charge of reconstruction and housing that the GDR authorities had said that 'Dresden needs neither churches nor baroque buildings' and that in 1963 the oldest church in the city was blown up. Not surprisingly, it became a symbol of resistance to be in favour of restoring

Dresden's famous landmarks. Now, a properly balanced
city plan is being produced which will draw strength from
Dresden's great historical tradition and preserve as well as
modernize. We were taken to see the progress on the
reconstruction of the palace of the Saxon kings by a city
official, a young *Ossi* woman whose abrupt manner was
somewhat reminiscent of the old GDR. The palace was a
vast building site, though one glorious baroque façade had
been restored. It would obviously not be before the next
century that it was completed. Afterwards, we wandered
into the Zwinger pleasure garden, designed by Matthäus
Daniel Pöppelmann for the Electors of Saxony and rebuilt
during the GDR period, where crowds including both West
German and foreign tourists were lingering in the afternoon
sun. Two teenage girls, one on the cello and the other on the
violin, were playing Bach. An open violin case in front of
them was already filling up with marks. Baroque Dresden
was clearly re-emerging as one of Europe's glories, which
would help Saxony attract both tourists and investment.

Given all the uncertainty and change, it is difficult to
make an accurate assessment of the progress of the East
German economy. Economic experts point to high
growth rates over the last two years and predict a similar
expansion over the next few years. But, following the
virtual collapse in output in 1990–91, growth starts from
a low base. And, although there has been an improvement
in industrial production, the main motors of recovery are
the construction and service industries. East German manufacturing, once the pride of the Soviet bloc, has been
decimated and now represents only 4.5 per cent of total
German turnover in manufacturing. To an alarming
extent, the East German economy is still dependent on
transfers from West Germany. As the Frankfurt office of
Goldman Sachs puts it,

The structure of the East German economy is somewhat similar to what a retirement community would create, with a strong emphasis – and dependence – on the supply of goods and services for local needs. Without the transfers from West Germany, the demand for non-traded (and traded) goods would crumble – and the East German expansion would go into reverse.

In the former GDR, the Treuhand, the agency which has privatized East Germany's huge and inefficient state owned industries, is criticized for its role in the collapse of East Germany's manufacturing industry. Even Norbert Walter, the influential and conservative chief economist of the Deutsche Bank, talked to me about 'the organized de-industrialization of East Germany'. The statistics are staggering. In under four years, the Treuhand has sold off almost 13,500 firms. But in most instances, getting firms ready for privatization involved radical restructuring and, usually, massive redundancies. Only about 20 per cent of the privatized firms were sold to East Germans, mostly through management buy-outs. There is little doubt that the Treuhand has masterminded the quickest and most comprehensive transformation to a market economy in the whole of the former Soviet bloc. But the question remains whether this change was carried out too speedily, too ruthlessly and sometimes even corruptly. I well remember talking with a Conservative peer and former adviser to Tory Chancellors of the Exchequer on a plane coming back from Dresden in 1991. His considered judgement was that the tough approach of the Treuhand, coming on top of other adverse factors such as the 1 to 1 monetary union, the collapse of eastern markets and the wages surge, was bound to lead to mass unemployment and social discontent. Today well over a million East German workers are unemployed, while some further two million are classified as on short-time, retraining or job-creation schemes. In Brandenburg, the spokesman of the SPD-led Land Government, Erhard

Thomas, a former West German journalist, told us, 'We are losing more jobs than we are creating. Official statistics are a mere fiction – 1 out of 2 are unemployed or on a special programme.' He added: 'The basic mood is almost at an explosive level.' What was being said is that 'they promised us democracy – they gave us the free market with all its problems.' It was true that the unemployed benefit from West German social security but costs have gone up. 'It is a two thirds, one third society, with one third being badly off.' He added that the decline in the birthrate – 55 per cent down on 1989 – and the 40 per cent jump in the divorce rate is evidence of a society in trauma.

In Potsdam, we discussed the winners and losers in the new East Germany with the head of the Brandenburg SPD *fraction* office, a *Wessi* from North Rhein-Westphalia. He informed us that

> the losers are those who used to work in big firms – they have not only lost their jobs but all the social protection and perks which went with their jobs. The winners are those who work in construction, service industries or the professions. Builders, bankers, doctors and car insurance salesmen have done well out of unification.

He pointed out that '*die Wende*' happened all at once and affected everyone.

> The problems are not just economic – they are psychological too. People have lost not only their jobs but their self respect. The Communists said capitalism was uncaring. To some extent, they have been proved right.

One evening in Leipzig, we met both the winners and losers. We paid £25 to hear Kurt Masur's orchestra play Bruch's Violin Concerto and Beethoven's *Eroica* at the Gewandhaus. Like most conductors, Masur is something of a showman with the added bonus of romantic good looks. Of course, after his brave leadership in Leipzig in 1989, he is also an East German hero whom many in the East would have liked to have seen as President. The concert goers were smart and middle-class, with the women as well dressed as they would be in the West. In contrast, after the opulence of the concert we ate schnitzels and drank the local beer in the still run-down Hauptbahnhof. We spotted our first skinheads, who were somewhat inebriated but, by British standards, pretty tame. One came over to us and asked us for the price of a beer. Very conscious of our exposed role as well heeled foreigners, we coughed up.

East German resentment at what has happened to their economy is exacerbated by what they perceive, with considerable justice, to be a West German 'takeover' of the East. A number of factors combined together to ensure that unification would mean a Western takeover. These included the adoption of Article 23 of the West German Basic Law as the method of union, under which the former GDR had to adopt the whole of the Federal Republic's laws, regulations, procedures and institutions; the collapse of East German industry and the sale of most of its privatized remnants to *Wessis*; the discrediting of thousands of East German politicians, managers, bureaucrats, and academics because of links with the Stasi and the old regime; and the flood of *Wessi* equivalents driven eastwards by a potent mixture of duty, ambition, and opportunity. The press officer of the Berlin City economics and technology department, himself a West Berliner, put it bluntly. 'After all, you must expect changes when a successful company merges with an unsuccessful one.' Dr Hanna-Renate Laurien, the CDU Speaker of the Berlin parliament, who reminded us of a more sympathetic version of Mrs Thatcher, said it was sad but inevitable that *Ossis* should feel second class citizens – but the help of *Wessis* was needed to organize and run the new democratic Länder. She spoke like the better kind of imperialist, full of sympathy for the *Ossis* but believing that they had a great deal to learn.

Everywhere we went we found West Germans running or helping to run the show. In Schwerin, capital of the new Land of Mecklenburg-Vorpommern, a beautiful city with a spectacular neo-gothic castle and surrounded by lakes, we had an appointment with the CDU Minister-President of the new Land in his fine eighteenth-century offices. While we awaited his arrival, we were briefed by two *Wessi* officials, Kurt Stockel, a retired professional diplomat now foreign affairs adviser, and Thomas Ellerbeck, the deputy press attaché. Ellerbeck told us that he had come east because he felt that he had a duty to help. It was very exciting 'being involved in building things up from scratch'. But the East could eventually assist the West. According to Ellerbeck, the 'can-do' experience in the East would help in loosening things up in the old Federal Republic.

An hour late, the Minister-President, Dr Berndt Seite, came rushing in. Seite is an *Ossi*, a Lutheran veterinary surgeon, who was a member of the Church Senate. We had heard about the accusations of him being involved with the Stasi and about a succession of ministerial resignations from the Land government. We knew that he had been all afternoon before a Landtag Committee on a waste disposal issue which had already caused the resignation of the Environment Minister. Yet, though under severe pressure, he had a refreshingly unpompous manner and a nice smile. As a prominent churchman, Seite would have obviously had contacts with the regime, so much so that he was able to go to a Boston conference as a church representative. He said that he was pushed into politics by the events of 1989 in order to 'bring about the new system'. He was at first a member of New Forum but quickly realized that he needed to be a member of one of the West German parties if 'you wanted to change things'. Most of his former church colleagues joined the SPD but he thought that too many former Communists were becoming members, so he decided to join the CDU (which was a fellow-travelling party). He emphasized what an enormous change '*die Wende*' was: 'Everybody's life is changed by it.' But he had confidence in the *Ossis*: 'They are a very robust people.' I realized that his political advantage was that he had *not* been a professional politician – and that he understood what the *Ossis* were going through because he had himself lived through their experience. He seemed to be a difficult man for the SPD to beat. At the Land election in October 1994, the CDU held on to their vote and, after protracted negotiations, Seite remained as Minister-President, heading a CDU–SPD coalition.

In Brandenburg, which was SPD run, we met *Wessi* officials from an SPD stronghold in the West – North Rhine Westphalia. Intriguingly, perhaps because the Minister-President, Manfred Stolpe, himself an *Ossi*, was a strong character, and because the SPD had been in opposition nationally, they were more sensitive to Eastern resentments. 'The impact of unification has been an enormous psychological blow to many *Ossis*,' they told us. At the Dom Café in the close of the redbrick Brandenburg Cathedral, we met Dr Hans-Otto Bräutigam, Stolpe's Minister of Justice, a former UN ambassador and representative of the Federal Republic in East Berlin who was brought in by Stolpe to clean up the 'law and order' system in the Land. Bräutigam was appointed by Stolpe because he was a personal friend and knew the former East German system. He told us how he cleaned up the judicial system. The criteria were: i) had the judges violated human rights? ii) had they had a genuine change of heart? iii) did they have

political responsibilities or hold political office in the past?
iv) what were they like as human beings? By these criteria,
over 50 per cent of judges were deemed unacceptable; 70
per cent of those acceptable were under thirty-five. They
all had to be retrained. As to the police, it was very
difficult: 'What do you do with the police in a police
state?' Ninety per cent of the police were still there but
they were being retrained. He reminded us that the Federal
Republic was policed by 'democrats who only became
democrats after 1945'. As to youth extremism, Bräutigam
said this was an all-German, not just an East German
problem. However, 'as a German Minister, I have to take
youth extremism more seriously.' He was referring to the
German past – and to the fact that the 'hooligans' used
Nazi slogans and that racial hatred was being stirred up
again. 'There is no doubt life in the East has become more
unstable following *die Wende*.' His last word was that
'There is a lot of aggression in the country as people realize
how difficult – and different – things are.' We had heard
the authentic voice of modern liberal Germany.

After the meeting with Dr Bräutigam, we were taken to
a 'Europe day' reception in the fine red brick cathedral
cloisters to meet Manfred Stolpe. Stolpe is a controversial
figure, the former lay spokesman of the Protestant Church
who acted as a go-between between the Church and the
Communist regime. Stasi files seemed to indicate that
Stolpe had been too close to the Communists, though
there is no evidence that he had ever betrayed anyone. On
the contrary, it is clear that he greatly assisted a number of
dissidents and conscientious objectors. In the East, the
accusations made against Stolpe seemed to have added to
rather than detracted from his popularity. He was triumphantly re-elected in September 1994. Stolpe told me that
a lot of British firms had expressed interest in investing or
had invested in Brandenburg – and mentioned the example

of Ready Mix. He was also at pains to let me know that he was encouraging good relations with Poland – economic success in Poland was good news for Brandenburg, as it would discourage migrants. He said that there were ten million Polish visitors a year and that German children were being encouraged to learn Polish in schools. Stolpe was a wild card but I was not surprised that he was so popular. He was the leading *Ossi* politician because he understood better than anyone what the *Ossis* had lived through and how they felt now.

But for every Stolpe and Seite, there were far more *Wessis* in top positions in politics, administration and business. An SPD Saxon Landtag MP who, like Kurt Biedenkopf, the CDU Land Minister-President, came from the West in 1990, commented, 'East Germany is now a colony of the West. Every organization in East Germany has been taken over by the West Germans and that includes the unions as well as industry and government.'

Erhard Thomas described the new Länder to us as 'a society in trauma'. This was due not only to mass unemployment and to the end of free kindergarten and child care facilities which, under the GDR, provided the essential support for working women. It was due, above all, to the rapidity of change and the loss of self respect and identity.

Resentment and discontent has alarmingly spilled over into violence and attacks on foreigners. In August 1992, gangs of extremist youths, shouting 'Germany for the Germans' and cheered on by crowds of local people, attacked and set on fire a Rostock refugee centre which housed Romanies and Vietnamese. This incident led to a week of demonstrations and counter-demonstrations in Rostock by neo-Nazi extremists and their democratic opponents. We spoke a year later to the Rostock official in charge of race relations who had, by all accounts, shown great personal courage by leading some of the Vietnamese to safety during the riots. He blamed the media for 'one-sided reporting' and claimed that Rostock was by no means xenophobic – indeed, as a port, it is 'very accustomed to welcoming foreigners'. He also said that racialist feelings had been whipped up by *Wessis*, including the Prime Minister of Bavaria, and that outsiders had been responsible for much of the violence. He did, however, admit that unemployment was high in the block of flats where the violence occurred, that the big expansion of asylum seekers, particularly gypsies, in Rostock was resented and that procedures locally had been 'exhausted'. Later, the mayor of Rostock resigned after the publication of an official report which castigated the Town Hall's handling of the disturbances.

But, despite the worrying numbers of racist incidents, support for right-wing extremist parties in the East has been very low. The real beneficiary of social discontent has not been the extremist right but the successor to the former East German Communist Party – the Party of Democratic Socialism (PDS). With its parliamentary group led by George Gysi, a personable lawyer in his forties who, under the old regime, defended dissidents, the PDS polled consistently well in the super election year of 1994, including winning 20 per cent in the European elections and just under 20 per cent in the October federal elections.

The main reason for the PDS's success seems clear. As an *Ossi* economist from Brandenburg put it to me, 'At least the PDS is an East German party' and as such is best placed to benefit from disillusionment with the CDU performance in the East over the last few years. An agriculturalist from Halle said, 'If the *Wessis* treat us like poor country cousins then that motivates us to vote for the party of poor country cousins, the PDS.' In contrast to the SPD, which is still very weak organizationally, the PDS still retains something of its old structure, enabling it to communicate more effectively with Eastern voters. So long as social discontent persists, the PDS is likely to remain a political force in the east.

The key to East Germany's future and to the success of unification is sustained industrial recovery. Sooner rather than later, East Germany must start to manufacture things again, even if the processes and the goods produced are very different from those of the old GDR. It may be that, if the West German recovery from the recession is sustained over the next few years, there could be a relatively quick and self sustainable upturn in the East. On the other hand, if the recovery in the West is shallow or falters, then the East German economy could continue to be little more than a market for West German goods – a recipe for instability.

The social, political and psychological condition of the new Länder is clearly linked to and just as important as the economic. The outbreaks of extremist and racial violence against foreigners are worrying, even if they have been exaggerated. And the opinion polls and the substantial vote for the PDS throughout 1994 show that the *Ossis* are well aware and increasingly resentful of their colonial status vis-à-vis the West. There is also the sheer lack of experience in the East of democratic attitudes and procedures to be considered. Their only democratic school has been the short and unsuccessful Weimar period: otherwise their role models are the Kaiser, Adolf Hitler, and Walter Ulbricht and Erich Honecker. However, it may be true, as Dr Berndt Seite said to us, that East Germans are a 'robust people' used to putting up with hardship, and they are probably more optimistic about the medium-term future than their *Wessi* counterparts.

The last important question about the new Länder is just

how long the *Wessis* will continue to underwrite the East German economy. At the minimum, the West is paying DM 150 billion a year to the East — a vast transfer of wealth which is being largely funded by the West German taxpayer. If this transfer is discontinued or substantially reduced, then the consequences in the East could be dire. My view is that the Germans will succeed in transforming the East, but it is going to take much longer than anyone thought — at least until the end of the decade — and will depend on West Germany being prepared to continue to pay for the East. That has implications not only for Germans but also for the rest of us Europeans.

# Chapter Three

## WESTERN RESENTMENT:
## PAYING THROUGH THE NOSE

*Bonn researcher*: 'Unification is a wonderful challenge for Germany'

*Hamburg bus driver*: 'As a *Wessi*, I am prepared to pay something for the East but the *Ossis* should not expect the fruit of forty years of West German hard work without having earned it'

These two comments reflect the mixed feelings in West Germany about unification now that the *Wessis* understand that they are going to have to underwrite the East German economy at least until the end of the decade. The initial optimism, so sedulously fostered by the German Government, quickly gave way to uncertainty, disappointment and even resentment. The public mood of pessimism was exacerbated by an eighteen-month recession, the longest since the war, which drove up unemployment in West Germany to over two-and-a-half million, as well as by an explosion of refugees and immigrants and by a dramatic increase in attacks on foreigners. For much of the period after the 1990 federal elections, voters reacted against the main established parties, either by voting for smaller parties or by not voting at all.

In spring 1990, the Federal German ambassador, Baron Hermann von Richthofen, a relative of the Red Baron, the First World War flying ace, came to a room on the Committee Corridor of the House of Commons to give the Treasury Select Committee a briefing on the costs of unification. The ambassador was one of the most charming, intelligent and skilful diplomats ever to represent his

country in Britain. Even so, he appeared remarkably com-
placent, even unrealistic. In response to questions, he told
us that there was 'no need for tax increases or special levies
to finance German unification'. The resources needed
would come from economic growth and 'a temporary
increase in net borrowing'. The ambassador argued that
higher taxes would be counter-productive because they
would choke off growth and 'reduce the need for strict
budgetary discipline both in the Federal Republic and in
the GDR'. While accepting there would be adjustment
problems in the GDR, he predicted that unification would
trigger a growth 'bonanza' which would benefit not only
the two Germanies but the Federal Republic's European
partners as well.

It would be, of course, unfair to blame the German
ambassador for his over-optimistic briefing. He was merely
speaking from a brief prepared for him by the Ministry of
Finance and echoing the views of the German Chancellor.
A few weeks earlier, Helmut Kohl had given an interview
to David Marsh of the *Financial Times* in which he had
painted an astonishingly glowing picture of the impact of
unification on the East German economy. He said

> I wouldn't know the Germans if there was not to be straight
> away an enormous car boom. The Germans have a tendency
> towards eating, drinking, cars and travel as the priorities. And
> when the East Germans have a lot of cars, then, of course, they
> will need repairing. Then there will be an incredible push in
> construction . . . In East Germany you have the highest popula-
> tion of working women – 90 per cent. So you have two
> incomes. And what does the wife say, 'At last I want a decent
> bathroom' – just like in the magazines. And this will give a
> unique chance for the plumbers and handymen.[1]

Kohl's *Financial Times* interview illustrates clearly both his
strengths and weaknesses as a politician – on the one hand,
his ability to communicate in everyday language and

images, his bluff good humour and his belief in himself and in his policies; on the other hand, his over-simplifications, his facile optimism about unification and his eye for the political main chance. In his defence it should be said that almost every expert in Western Europe overestimated the efficiency of the 'clapped out' East German economy. As Robert Leicht, the editor of the liberal Hamburg weekly, *Die Zeit*, put it in 1993,

> We made the assumption that the two strongest societies in the East and West were uniting and that unification would be successful in a relatively short time – say five years. The reality was very different – you were actually combining an extremely rich and a quite poor society – and that is why unification will take at least a generation.[2]

At the time, Kohl's political opponents, above all Oskar Lafontaine, the SPD Chancellor candidate in 1990, rightly argued that unification would be expensive and would inevitably involve increases in taxes. Paradoxically it was a message that German voters might have been prepared to accept from Kohl. The problem for the SPD was that the party had lost credibility because, with the exception of Willy Brandt, it had been lukewarm about unification. It was all too easy for the Christian Democrats to say, 'The Social Democrats got it wrong about unification. Why should anybody listen to them when they start carping about its costs?' A year later, Otto Schlecht, State Secretary at the Economics Ministry, admitted that:

> We deceived ourselves about the size and depth of the restructuring crisis. We gave prominence to the positive elements and forced the negative ones into the background. This was because we wanted people to take heart – and because there was an election campaign.[3]

At the end of October 1992, Hermann von Richthofen again gave the Treasury Select Committee a briefing, this time in the splendid German embassy in Belgrave Square.

We were about to go to Frankfurt to see officials of the
Bundesbank, following 'Black Wednesday', 16 September
1992, when Britain was forced out of the Exchange Rate
Mechanism (ERM), in part as a consequence of high
German interest rates and the impact of unification on the
German economy.

The ambassador's message was a sombre one – very
different from that which he had delivered to us in 1990.
He admitted that East German output, so far from expanding as he had predicted, had actually fallen by almost half,
while employment had dropped by a third. He explained
this sudden and catastrophic collapse by the lack of competitiveness of East German industry, whose productivity was
only a third of its West German counterpart but whose
wages were now 70 per cent of West German levels, and
by the fall off in trade with Eastern Europe. As we pointed
out to him, he should also have mentioned the 1 to 1
monetary union. He went on to tell us how the costs of
unification had escalated. In 1992, the Eastern Länder had
received DM 160 billion from the Federal budget, mostly
to finance unemployment and other social security benefits.
Much of these subsidies to the East were supported by
borrowing which had massively increased the budget deficit. But the West German taxpayer was also making a very
substantial contribution to propping up East German consumption and was likely to have to continue doing so for a
very long time to come. What was even more disturbing
was that the West German economy was itself facing a
downturn.

On our visit to Frankfurt a few days later, it was made
clear to us that, if anything, the ambassador had been
underplaying the deterioration in the German economy. In
part because of the rift between the British Government
and the Bundesbank (see Chapter 7), the Treasury Select
Committee was received with great courtesy by the Presi-

dent and Vice-President of the Bundesbank, Helmut Schlesinger and Hans Tietmeyer, and by their officials in their
1960s building on the outskirts of the city. Most of our
discussions were devoted to the events surrounding 'Black
Wednesday' and the implications for the ERM and for
European economic and monetary union, but they stressed
to us the difficult economic situation in Germany. Consistently less sanguine than the Government about unification,
they underlined that there was unlikely to be any self-
sustaining recovery in the East for a long time.

The Bundesbank officials remained sceptical about the
government's ability to bring the ballooning budget deficit
under control. They reminded us that it was their legal
obligation to safeguard the currency and explained patiently
that it was their concern about rising inflation in Germany
following unification which had led them to put up interest
rates to record levels. Only if they believed that inflation
was safely down to 2 per cent would they bring interest
rates down. The Deutsche Bank was even blunter. On the
top floor of their fine glass headquarters, we were told by
Norbert Walter, their chief economist, that the West
German economy 'had fallen off a cliff'. The high interest
rates imposed by the Bundesbank had choked off the
immediate post-unification boom in the West German
economy, as the *Ossis* spent their DMs as if there was no
tomorrow (in this, if in nothing else about the economic
impact of unification, Helmut Kohl was proved right). On
top of a fall in demand at home, the revaluation of the D-
Mark against the currencies of some of its trading partners,
including Britain, following 'Black Wednesday', had made
German goods uncompetitive in a number of key markets,
while the impact of high German interest rates on other
countries such as France had also decreased demand for
German exports. As if this was not enough, German industry, we were told, was suffering for the first time from

long-term 'structural problems'. In the past, innovation
and quality had enabled Germany to survive downturns –
now they faced competition from countries like Japan and
the new 'Asian tigers'. A month earlier Helmut Kohl had
been forced to admit, in a speech to the Bundestag, that
Germany was in trouble: 'We know today better than we
knew two years ago that this truly secular, unique event
brings with it huge problems, more than many – including
myself – had expected.'

Both 1992 and 1993 were difficult years for the Germans.
As it became obvious that the West Germans were going
to have to finance the East German economy for many
years, West Germany itself went into recession, output
dropped and unemployment soared. Famous industrial
firms, like Bosch, Volkswagen, Daimler-Benz and Opel,
cut costs by making thousands redundant and putting
other workers on short time. Over a million jobs were lost
in the West between 1992 and 1994.

At the Anglo-German conference which took place in
March 1993 at Königswinter, the attractive nineteenth-century watering spa near Bonn on the right bank of the
Rhine, I learnt from my German friends about the strains
which the combination of unification, recession, and immigration were putting on German society. Not surprisingly,
Western attitudes towards the East had become more
ambivalent.

I watched an episode of a controversial German TV
sitcom, '*Motzki*'. Motzki is a fat, grumbling, foul-mouthed
retired driving school instructor who lives in a run-down
working-class neighbourhood of West Berlin. He thinks
that unification is a catastrophe and rants against all East
Germans – including his sister-in-law. *Ossis* are idle, greedy
and ungrateful scroungers who 'since childhood have been
used to living off other people'. He is convinced that they
are after his money. Many *Ossis* found the programme

highly offensive and a number of politicians, including the Prime Minister of Baden-Württemberg, called for the series to be withdrawn. The producers, however, argued that, by ridiculing *Wessi* prejudices, the series would help to overcome rather than widen East-West divisions. The accuracy of its description of *Wessi* views was confirmed by a poll in *Der Spiegel* which showed that 70 per cent of West Germans thought that East Germans were idle. More disturbing than Motzki's prejudices was the dramatic growth in racist violence by neo-Nazis, especially but not exclusively in the Eastern Länder (see p. 35–36). Although the numbers of such attacks had been rising rapidly (there were 2,000 in 1992), it took the burning to death of a Turkish grandmother and her two daughters in November 1992 at Mölln, a sleepy market town in Schleswig-Holstein, to awaken the political establishment to the threat from the extremist right. A number of neo-Nazi organizations were banned. The office for the Defence of the Constitution established a special unit to counter neo-Nazi activity, and a new package of policing and protective measures was announced. Equally important, there were massive popular demonstrations, including candlelight processions in Munich, Hamburg, Cologne, Frankfurt, Hanover, Bonn and in Mölln itself. As the foreign editor of the *Süddeutsche Zeitung* wrote, 'at last the silent majority is standing up for decency and democracy.'[4]

In the special session on racism and immigration held at the Königswinter Conference, we were told by our German colleagues that, since unification, there had been over two million extra immigrants joining the 4.5 million 'guest' workers already there. These immigrants were mainly either 'asylum seekers' from the former Yugoslavia or Eastern Europe under the extremely liberal Article 16 of the Basic Law, or ethnic Germans from Poland, Romania or the Soviet Union taking up their rights under the

Constitution to settle in Germany. 'The explosion in the number of immigrants against the background of unification and recession is providing an ideal breeding ground for xenophobia,' said a German participant. All the political parties agreed that the asylum laws had to be changed – Germany had the most liberal asylum law in Europe. On the other hand, it also had, as the Turks had discovered, inflexible laws of citizenship. These would need to be changed as well. As a German journalist put it, 'Candles are one thing; rights are another.'

At Königswinter in March 1993, I learnt a new word – *Politikverdrossenheit*, or weariness with politics. In Land and local elections, German voters were turning against the established parties and either voting for smaller parties, including the extremist right and the PDS, or not bothering to vote at all. In June 1992, the Federal President, Richard von Weizsäcker, had given the political establishment a terrific ticking off, accusing them of being power mad but 'absent minded' when carrying out their responsibilities.

In addition, it seemed as if the Germans were going cool on European union, or at least on a single currency, if it meant replacing their beloved D-Mark. This was depressing news for a strongly pro-European Labour MP who had just come from extolling the virtues of a European Bank to a somewhat sceptical House of Commons. I had at least hoped that the Germans, who, with the French, were the main architects of the Maastricht Treaty, would stand firm.

All in all, there was a mood of angst amongst my German friends. Business people complained about high labour costs and taxes, trade unionists worried about unemployment, politicians felt defensive and only the journalists enjoyed the bad news. Former SPD Chancellor Helmut Schmidt, in a wide-ranging jeremiad of a book published at that time, castigated both Government and opposition alike for the failures over unification.[5] His loudest brickbats were, however, reserved for Helmut Kohl. Though giving him credit for having grasped the opportunity of unification, he was highly critical of his conduct afterwards. 'Practically everything else which Kohl undertook after 3 October 1990, the date of German unity, was partly wrong, partly mistaken, too hesitant and too late.' He concluded: 'Our position is in no way satisfactory. We have made serious mistakes and we are placing ourselves in further danger through prejudice, egotism and sloth.'

That winter, I was able to test the German temperature again. In February 1994, I went on a superbly organized lecture tour for the Deutsch-Englische Gesellschaft, mainly in the most populous Land, North Rhine-Westphalia. The subject of my talk was German unification. Despite the difficulties, I expressed confidence that Germany would eventually succeed in bringing its two parts together economically, socially and psychologically, and, in reply to the question 'Is German unification a good thing for Europe?' I gave a positive answer. Not surprisingly, my audiences liked the 'medium-term' optimism of my message but were still anxious about what was happening in both West and East.

It was snowing heavily both in Essen, formerly a mining and steel city in the heart of the Ruhrgebiet now transformed into a shopping and service centre, and in Münster, the city where the Treaty of Westphalia, which ended the Thirty Years War, was signed by the Catholic negotiators in 1648. Those who came to listen to me were mostly the professional middle class. They did not complain about paying taxes for the East. They did feel, however, that the Government had wildly underestimated the economic problems and they were also concerned about rising unemployment and the incidents of racism. When I argued that

Germany should now assume a greater leadership role in
Europe and the world, there were a number of dissenters.
In Essen, a female urban planner in her thirties was against
using German troops in any kind of interventionist role,
while in Münster a middle-aged teacher said, 'It will take a
long time for us to become normal again.' The wife of my
host in Münster summed up the mood when she commented, 'I am glad that we are taking a long time to make
up our minds: it shows that we take democratic debate –
and our past – seriously.'

In Bielefeld, a textile town and formerly British Army
headquarters in Germany, I learnt about the difficulties
which a medium sized family textile firm was experiencing
during the recession, especially over high labour costs and
corporate taxes. The managing director and his board
members told me that, as part of the process of restructuring, they had had to make some of their employees redundant, so it seemed that the workers – and society – were
paying for the restructuring of German industry. I made
one foray into what some *Wessis* call 'the wild East' by
smooth, comfortable and very punctual express trains to
Magdeburg. Magdeburg has a bloody past. To Protestant
outrage, it was brutally sacked by the imperialist forces
under Tilly in 1631 during the Thirty Years War and was
badly bombed by the Allies in 1945. Under the GDR, it
had the reputation of being a drab industrial centre. Now
its prospects are looking up, as it has become the capital of
the Land of Sachsen-Anhalt and its splendid nineteenth-
century streets are being restored.

At Magdeburg, I learnt how divided Germany really
was. The decent, high-minded *Ossi* civil servant who was
responsible for universities in the Land administration and
who accompanied me during my stay was insistent that
'We are all just Germans, not *Ossis* or *Wessis*.' Yet he
admitted that he felt and thought differently from the

*Wessis* who were working alongside him. Under the pressure of adversity, there had been a sense of community. Now that was vanishing. I spoke to his friend, the arts editor of a local newspaper who came from Heidelberg, who told me, 'They are different – it is a different country. To begin with, I felt like a foreign correspondent.' The owners of the small and very comfortable family hotel in which I stayed were a young couple from Frankfurt am Main. The hotel had originally belonged to the husband's family. The couple had claimed back the home which the family had left when they fled to the West. His wife told me that they saw themselves as escaping from the rat race in the West, providing themselves with jobs for life in the East (if, as seems very likely, the hotel is a success), and giving themselves 'a sense of mission'. Yet, because most of the hotel's customers are business people from the West, they seldom meet Easterners. Like the arts editor from Heidelberg, they were foreigners in their own country.

While I was in Germany, a poll was published in *Der Spiegel* which showed that 82 per cent of East Germans thought that Easterners were second class citizens, while 64 per cent of West Germans disagreed. At the same time 76 per cent of the Easterners considered that Bonn was not doing enough to help; by contrast, the majority of Westerners thought that enough was being done and 46 per cent believed that the costs of unification were too high.[6] According to a *Der Spiegel* poll in December 1993, only 10 per cent of East Germans and 20 per cent of West Germans feel themselves as belonging to a common people. It was sadly very clear that, despite unification, 'the wall in people's minds' was as strong as ever. The division between West Germany and East Germany was likely to remain for a considerable time.

In Bonn, my friend and companion of many Königswinter Conferences, Karl Kaiser, the director of the German

Institute for International Affairs, explained it this way:
'Germany is bigger, yes – but in terms of per capita
income it is poorer and it is certainly more divided than
before.' Karl, who is a formidable and lucid interpreter of
Germany to the world, said that Germany was a 'laboratory
for change'. There was massive change in the East – and at
the same time radical restructuring going on in the West.
He argued that there was, in fact, an unofficial consensus
between the CDU and the SPD on the need for reforms
in welfare and fiscal policy and pointed to the 'solidarity'
package of spending cuts and income tax increases to help
pay for the costs of unification negotiated between the
parties in March 1993 and the agreement to change the
asylum laws as evidence for his propositions. Underlying
his remarks was a quiet confidence that federal German
institutions, procedures and methods would prove capable
of making a success of unification.

By June 1994 the mood in West Germany was beginning
to change. Together with two leading British journalists
and the London head of the Ebert *Stiftung*, the think-tank
attached to the SPD, I had a week of meetings with
Government and Land ministers and officials, bankers,
industrialists, trade unionists and economic experts in Bonn,
Cologne, Frankfurt and Munich. In Germany, June is the
asparagus season and everywhere we went we ate long and
thick white asparagus with mayonnaise, and listened to a
message which, if it was not as 'upbeat' as CDU politicians
claimed, was much more optimistic than it had been in
1992 and 1993.

It was clear that there were formidable problems still
facing Germany. Dr Joachin Grünewald, the Parliamentary State Secretary at the Federal Ministry of Finance,
summed some of these up with a frankness that many of
his other parliamentary colleagues might well have emu-

lated. Unification had reduced Germany's GDP per head, taking the country from second to sixth in the European Union in terms of wealth per capita. Five per cent of German GDP was now going to the Eastern Länder in transfers – and this kind of subsidy would have to continue until at least the end of the decade. Transfers amounted to a quarter of the Federal budget, so that one in four of every DM spent was going to the East. The recession had been the deepest since the war – the consequential rise in unemployment benefit expenditure and shortfall in tax revenue had increased the public deficit by DM 30 billion. The burden of social costs and taxes remained too heavy for industry; 'Germany is still a high tax, high cost country,' Dr Grünewald told us.

At the Federal Ministry of Labour and Social Affairs, Dr Werner Tegtmeier, the Permanent Under-Secretary of State, underlined the human cost of transformation to a market economy in the East and recession and restructuring in the West. Three-and-a-half million jobs had been lost in the new Länder, while, in West Germany, one million jobs had gone. He also stressed that, in East Germany, in addition to the 1.5 million unemployed, two million more were on labour schemes which were being mostly financed by Government funds. He also said that the German labour market and social facilities had had to cope with two million refugees since unification. The IFO Economic Institute in Munich told us that 'the social costs of unemployment are being paid for by society.'

There were other challenges ahead. 'We have new Hong Kongs on our doorsteps,' was a constant refrain. In Munich we were reminded by Bavarian Land government officials that wage levels in neighbouring Czechoslovakia were a tenth of those in West Germany, posing a threat to traditional Bavarian industries, like textiles and ceramics. Yet Germany cannot afford to exclude goods from Eastern

Europe, otherwise it will face the prospect of mass immigration from those countries, with all the strains which that could create inside Germany.

But, despite all these difficulties, there were now definite signs of recovery in the West, while, in the East, output was picking up, though from a low level. In the West, there was what Helmut Schieber, a board member of the Bundesbank, called 'a typically German upswing', based on a rise in exports and the beginning of an increase in investment. Consumption, held back by unemployment, increases in insurance contributions and a fall in real wages, was still stagnant. Even so, in Munich, the public relations head of BMW told us that there was now 'a mood swing towards optimism'.

The massive deterioration in competitiveness, so marked in 1992, had been largely overcome by a radical restructuring of German industry. The bright economists of the employers' Research Institute in Cologne predicted that, by 1996, German unit labour costs would be down to the OECD average. According to the June 1994 IFO report, 'unit labour costs in the manufacturing sector are falling significantly under the twin influences of faster productivity growth and slower wage growth.'[7] In plain language, the shedding of labour and restraint in wages have helped to bring down costs. But there has also been, according to both employers and unions as well as more impartial observers, the widespread adoption of new working methods, the development of new products and the discovery of new markets. 'West German industry really has done a good job,' said Norbert Walter of Deutsche Bank.

From a British perspective, what is so striking is that this restructuring has been achieved, to a considerable extent, through consultation with unions and works councils. In other words, the German social market consensus model, so derided by British Conservatives, has proved capable of adapting to change. We were told by IG Metall research officers in their modern offices at Frankfurt, 'If we are to retain our labour and social protection then we have to assist in increasing productivity.' Their counterparts in the employers' Economic Institute agreed that the unions had reacted very positively to the need to cut unit labour costs and assured us that 'the durability of the German social market consensus model is not in doubt', though further changes were needed. We were reminded of a number of trail-blazing agreements between employers and unions – for example at Volkswagen, and in the chemicals and engineering industries – which have restrained wage increases and introduced more flexible working practices in return for preserving jobs.

Politically the shift in the national mood proved a godsend to Chancellor Kohl. We had arrived on the night of Sunday 12 June 1994 to celebrate Labour and SPD victories in the European elections at the SPD headquarters in Bonn, only to find we were attending a wake as far as the Germans were concerned. The first exit polls just after 9 p.m. showed that the SPD was six points behind the CDU. The SPD Chancellor candidate, Rudolf Scharping, Prime Minister of the Rhineland-Palatinate Land Government, was immediately interviewed by TV commentators in party headquarters. Scharping, young looking, bearded and bespectacled, had the unenviable task of explaining the SPD's disappointing showing. He was dignified, polite and competent. He blamed the poor turn-out in the West and the PDS's strong performance in the East. 'We must motivate our voters,' he said. On a nearby TV, I watched Kohl performing a similar, though much easier task. He was positively bursting with joy and his chins quivered with delight. He admitted to disappointment with the result of the FDP, his coalition partners, who failed to get the 5 per cent necessary to get into the European

Parliament. Referring to them as though they were his wayward teenage cousins, Kohl said, 'I will have to campaign hard for them in the October Federal elections.' After Kohl's mismanagement of unification, he did not deserve to win. But, in the Euro election, he had clearly benefited from the economic recovery; from Scharping's tactical error in giving the impression that the SPD's version of the 'solidarity' package's tax proposals would hit people at a lower level than was actually planned; and, to Kohl's credit, from his consistent European policy.

There is little doubt that Helmut Schmidt was right when he condemned German politicians, above all the German Government led by Chancellor Kohl, for big mistakes in their handling of the economic consequences of unification. These errors contributed to a virtual industrial collapse in the East and indirectly to recession in the West and, in so doing, accentuated the divisions between Easterners and Westerners. However, if Schmidt is entirely justified in criticizing Kohl for policy errors and omissions following unification, he is far too pessimistic about the ability of his fellow countrymen to make a success of unification.

The key issue will be whether the West Germans will be able to sustain their support for the East, while at the same time continuing to adapt their own methods and policies to rapid change. From the evidence of my visits to Germany and contacts with Germans since unification, I remain an optimist. Of course, there are many external and internal challenges facing Germany. These include intense industrial competition from Eastern Europe as well as the Pacific basin, the prospect of large-scale immigration if there is a breakdown in the former Soviet bloc area, persistently high levels of domestic unemployment, and, above all, the continuing divisions and differences between the two parts of Germany.

But Germany's pluses far outweigh its minuses. West Germany remains one of the richest societies on earth, with a high per capita income, a strong industrial base and formidably impressive systems of transport, housing, health, education and training. The Federal Republic's democratic institutions, its political, economic and social structures, and its cultural achievements remain enduring sources of strength. Despite all the angst and self-doubt of 1992–93, the Germans have both the flexibility to adapt to change within the existing democratic and consensus framework and the persistence to see unification through to a successful conclusion.

Part Two

# WHY BONN IS NOT WEIMAR

## Chapter Four

## TRIBAL GERMANY:
## THE STRENGTHS OF FEDERALISM

'There is something in the nature of Germans that
thrives under the tutelage of regionalism and that has, in
turn, fared less well under the auspices of the nation and
nationalism. Essentially, the German character can best
be described as "tribal", a state of mind and outlook on
life . . . that makes it easy to link hands, under a common
constitution, with like minded people of the German
language.'

*Thomas Kielinger in* Sixteen Tribes of Germany[1]

One of the main strengths of the Federal Republic has
been its federal system of government which allows a wide
autonomy for the Länder within an overall national framework. This decentralized structure has suited admirably the
remarkable variety of German life. It has its roots in
historical tradition. It protects liberties, encourages diversity, and promotes experimentation and growth. It facili-
tated unification by making it quicker for the GDR
to merge with the Federal Republic (Germany united by
the new Länder joining the Federal Republic) but also by
re-establishing the former East German Länder (abolished
by the GDR) as new foci of identity for Easterners. As
John Ardagh puts it in his excellent book on the Germans,
'Federalism comes naturally to the Germans.'[2] The question
now being asked by critics is whether the federalism which
has served West Germany so well since 1949 will continue
to be a source of strength in the unified Germany or
whether it needs modification.

When foreigners, especially the British, talk about the

Germans they often speak as if there were only one German national character. Yet the visitor to Germany quickly realizes that there are many different types of Germans and many Germanies. It was partly this variation and lack of uniformity to which Goethe and Schiller, writing at the end of the eighteenth century before the first unification, referred to in their poem published in *The Muses Almanach for the Year 1797.* 'Any hope of forming yourselves into a nation, Germans, is in vain; develop yourselves rather – you can do it – more freely as human beings.'

On my travels in Germany, I have been struck by the big regional differences. These may not be much greater than the difference between, say, a Scot and a Londoner. But they are kept alive by the federal system which under-pins regional diversity. The northern cities of Hamburg and Bremen look to the North Sea – to Scandinavia, Holland and Britain. Their people are blunt speaking, Protes-tant rather than Catholic, supporters of the SPD rather than the CDU. Helmut Schmidt, with his cutting intelli-gence and blue sailor cap, is recognizably a Hamburger. At the other end of Germany is baroque Munich, capital of Bavaria, close to the Alps and to Austria and Italy, and, especially in summer, with a hint of a southern city about it. Bavarians are supposed to be beer swilling, thigh slap-ping, pleasure loving, the southern Germans of the picture postcard and the calendar. The late Franz-Josef Strauss, with his bull neck and tub-thumping oratorical style, was very much the stage Bavarian.

Of course, generalizations, even regional ones, should not be carried too far. In fact, Munich is a sophisticated fashion, film and cultural centre, inhabited mostly by people who were not born in the city (many of them foreigners) and more often than not ruled by the SPD. The CSU, the Conservative Bavarian sister party of the CDU, draws its main strength from outside Munich, from the rural areas and smaller towns. Even in southern Germany, there are obvious distinctions between Catholic Bavarians and Protestant Swabians. The Swabians are said to be slow speaking, hard working, even austere. When I asked a Bavarian during a meeting at BMW headquarters at Munich what he thought of the Swabians, he replied, 'If the Swabians see a table with one person, they think it is a party.'

In the West, the Rhinelanders face towards France and the Benelux countries. They are traditionally wine (and beer) drinkers, and, like the Bavarians, Catholic. Cologne, the Rhineland's cultural and media capital with excellent art galleries and museums and a magnificent cathedral, is an old Roman city and has a friendly and lively atmosphere. In the East lies Berlin, chosen as the seat of government as well as the capital of the united Germany in June 1991. Berliners are *sui generis* – sharp, caustic and witty. It was typical of them that, though they were moved by and grateful for President Kennedy's famous '*Ich bin ein Berliner*' speech in June 1963, they also made fun of his phrase. Everybody knows what Kennedy meant, but his words, as Berliners pointed out, could also mean 'I am a jam doughnut.' There are other well-known differences. In Baden-Württemberg, the relaxed people of Baden feel close to the French, while their neighbours in Württemberg are industrious Swabians. In North Rhine-Westphalia, I was told that, historically, the northern Rhineland was Frankish and part of the Roman empire, while Westphalia was Saxon and fell outside it. Münster, an attractive university city, certainly felt distant from the Rhineland or the Ruhrgebiet. Westphalians are supposed to be reserved. It is said that a Westphalian has to eat a sack of salt with another person before he or she becomes a friend.

The divisions between West and East Germany are obvious and have been discussed earlier in the book. But, even within the former GDR, there are marked contrasts – for example between the slow-moving Mecklenburgers and the bustling Saxons. Mecklenburg-Vorpommern, made up of what was the Grand Duchy of Mecklenburg and the German rump of the ancient province of Pomerania (the rest went to Poland in 1945), is a land of lakes and forests. Saxony, with the Ruhrgebiet, was traditionally the industrial heartland of Germany. The Saxons tell this story about the Mecklenburgers: One Saxon: 'The Mecklenburgers don't realize the Wall is down.' Second Saxon: 'They don't realize it existed at all.'

Differences extend to language. The handbook which German Government departments and embassies give to foreigners points out that, though there is a common High German or *Hochdeutsch*, Germany has a wealth of dialects. If Mecklenburgers, Frisians, Swabians, Bavarians, even Berliners or citizens of Cologne, addressed one another in their native dialects, they would find it extremely difficult to understand each other. I was told by a *Wessi* who worked as a journalist in Halle that the GDR had developed words which he sometimes did not grasp.

It has often been said that a key to the understanding of the Germans is their devotion to their *Heimat* (literally, home). This was the title of Edgar Reitz's brilliant eleven-part television drama series (referred to later in the book) which I, like so many other Europeans, was gripped by in the 1980s. Through the fortunes of a family in the Hunsrück, a district east of the Mosel, Reitz explored the theme, so important to Germans, of 'belonging'. Very often the commitment is not so much, or not only, to a Land but to a much smaller area, district, small city or town. The strong German sense of community has an ancient history going back perhaps to the German tribes described so graphically in Tacitus's *Germania*, certainly to the decentralized arrangements of the medieval Holy

Roman Empire of the German nation and to the more than three hundred *Kleinstaaterei* (small states) of the later seventeenth and eighteenth centuries. Today *Heimatstadt* (home town) Germany is one of the building blocks of the Federal Republic.

When the Western Allies came to reconstruct Germany after the war, they sensibly set up the Länder first, before a central government was created. Indeed it was representatives of the Länder who came together in Bonn to make the Federal Republic's Constitution – the Basic Law of 1949 – by which West Germany became a federal state. The Allies, particularly the United States, insisted on a federal solution because they wanted to build in checks and counterbalances to prevent the re-emergence of a dictatorship. The model which they proposed has been highly successful, in part because it was in keeping with an older German tradition. Viewed historically, federalism has been the German way of maintaining the balance between the centre and the periphery, of preserving regional variety within an overall national framework.

The Holy Roman Empire was a federal structure, albeit one with a weak centre presiding uneasily over an extremely fragmented and complex collection of states, territories, principalities and cities. The German Confederation of 1815, set up after the defeat of Napoleon (who had abolished the Empire in 1806), was more a loose confederation of states but it still had a federal diet or parliament. The short-lived pan-German Frankfurt Parliament of 1848–49 voted for federalism. Even in 1871, when Bismarck created a united Germany under Prussian control, the constitution of the Reich was federal. The ill-fated Weimar Republic, set up in 1919, was a fully fledged federal democracy, with eighteen Länder. Significantly, one of Hitler's first acts on his assumption of the Chancellorship in 1933 was to remove the powers of the Länder and in 1934 he abolished the federal system altogether. 'The sovereign rights of the Länder are taken over by the Reich,' he decreed. Hitler well understood that federalism was incompatible with dictatorship. Following unification, the Federal Republic now has sixteen Länder. Of these, Bavaria and Saxony closely correspond to the former kingdoms. In Bavaria, it is common to hear people say, 'I am Bavarian first and German only second.' Both the Hitler regime and the GDR made every effort to snuff out the Saxon identity but, once the Land of Saxony was restored in 1990, its Landtag (or parliament) at its first meeting declared itself, like Bavaria, a Free State. The smallest Land, Saarland, has had the necessary cohesion to vote twice this century, the second time in 1957, for Germany rather than France. Hamburg and Bremen were once proudly independent Hanseatic city states. Some of the rest are more artificial constructs. Both North Rhine-Westphalia, the most populous Land, and Lower Saxony were created out of the former Prussian Land which covered nearly two thirds of Germany, while Baden-Württemberg, set up in 1952, was an amalgamation of Baden, Baden-Hohenzollern and Württemberg. The newly reconstituted city of Berlin has become a separate Land, faced with the massive tasks of uniting the two Berlins and of recreating itself as the capital of Germany. However, whatever the historical antecedents of individual Länder, there is overwhelming support, according to polling data, for the federal system.

Germany has been described as 'a single country with seventeen governments: one in Bonn and one in each of the sixteen states.'[3] Apart from Switzerland and Belgium, it has the most decentralized system of government in Europe. The Länder are responsible for the police, culture (which includes a broad range of subjects from education to broadcasting) and local government. Jointly with central

Government, they control civil and criminal law, labour law, road transport and some aspects of economic policy. Not only have the Länder the power to legislate in these areas of 'concurrent tasks' if central Government chooses not to do so. Perhaps more importantly, they also administer federal laws within their boundaries. Foreign policy, defence and foreign economic policy are the prerogative of central Government. Even so, under Maastricht legislation, the Länder have the right to reject by a two thirds majority any EU action which they deem to be intrusive, unfair or otherwise detrimental to their interests. They take their European responsibilities seriously, maintaining offices in Brussels and sending representatives to the European Union's Assembly of the Regions.

Every Land has its own parliament (Landtag), government and prime minister (Minister-President). Government offices and parliament buildings are usually very splendid indeed. Facing on to the Hofgarten in Munich is the Bavarian State Chancellery, commonly known as the Straussoleum (after Franz-Josef Strauss). The Bavarian Landtag is housed in the Maximilianeum, a grandiose nineteenth-century palace, while the Berlin Landtag meets in the spacious former Prussian Landtag, closed down in 1933. The Hessen Land government and parliament occupy the Stadtschloss in Wiesbaden, built for the Dukes of Nassau in the 1840s. A Land prime minister is usually a very considerable political figure. After he left the Government in Bonn in the 1960s, Strauss went back to Bavaria to become prime minister. Three SPD Chancellor candidates, Oskar Lafontaine, Rudolf Scharping and Johannes Rau, have all been Land prime ministers, while Kurt Biedenkopf, a leading CDU politician, is prime minister of Saxony. Some prominent political leaders prefer to stay in their Land rather than go to Bonn, 'a big fish in a small pond', as one Land prime minister's aide called his boss.

The Länder have an important direct influence at national level. The members of the upper house (the Bundesrat) are appointed by the Länder governments as their representatives, voting *en bloc* as a delegation according to the colour(s) of the Land government. The Bundesrat is as much a gathering of state governments as a second chamber. The Federal Government must always submit bills first to the Bundesrat, but its consent is only necessary in the case of constitutional amendments (requiring a two thirds majority in the Bundesrat) and of laws affecting the powers and revenues of the Länder. However, the significance of this obligation is shown by the statistic that half of all federal legislation consists of 'consent' laws. The Bundesrat is also entitled to object to any law, though this objection can be overruled by a majority in the Bundestag. Members of the Bundesrat can attend and speak at all meetings of the Bundestag and its committees. For example, I heard Rudolf Scharping, who, though then not a member of the Bundestag, was, as Minister-President of the Rhineland-Palatinate, a member of the Bundesrat, speak powerfully on unemployment in the Bundestag.

The basic argument for federalism is one of freedom. It provides the maximum amount of regional autonomy and acts as a counterbalance to the centralizing tendencies of national governments. At the same time, as Germans and their admirers argue, it also promotes efficiency. Charles Handy, Irish management guru and social philosopher, puts it this way: 'Federalism is an age-old device for keeping the proper balance between big and small. Big in some things, small in others.'[4]

The key role played by the Länder in administration obviously helps in bringing government close to the people. If one lives in Bavaria, it is easier to go to Munich for an administrative decision or to see one's MP than to go to Bonn or, from 1998, to Berlin. In the Maximilianeum, where the Bavarian Landtag meets, I saw constituents dropping in to see their local MPs for advice. The popular support for Land government, the relatively high turnout in Land elections and the failure of any separatist movement to get off the ground all suggest that the majority of Germans believe that, on the whole, the system is working to their advantage.

Federalism also encourages devolution. The new capital, Berlin, comprises only about 4 per cent of the German population, compared to 15 per cent for Paris and London. Whereas in France and Britain many activities are concentrated in or around the capital, in Germany these are dispersed among more than half a dozen major cities. Norman Stone, Oxford Professor of Modern History, succinctly summed up the roles of the main cities of the old Federal Republic as follows: 'In fact, there are really six capitals besides Bonn – Munich for culture, Frankfurt for money, Düsseldorf for industry, Hamburg for commerce and eventually also West Berlin for sex.'[5] He could also have added Cologne for culture and the media and Stuttgart for Mercedes-Benz and high tech. In 1990 these Western cities were joined in the East by Dresden for culture and Leipzig for trade and books.

On a recent trip, I noted how much things are spread around. We went to Cologne to see the employers' federation, Düsseldorf to see the trade union federation, Bonn to see Government ministers and officials, Frankfurt to see the Bundesbank and the engineering union, IG Metall, and Munich to see BMW and the economic forecasting organization, IFO. If we had wanted to see the Constitutional Court, we would have had to go to Karlsruhe, while to visit the central employment office would have meant a trip to Nuremburg. In contrast to Britain and France, the media are also dispersed. The big weekly magazines, like *Die Zeit* and *Der Spiegel*, as well as Germany's '*Sun*', *Bild Zeitung*, are published in Hamburg. However, the *Frankfurter Allgemeine Zeiting* and the *Frankfurter Rundschau* are published in Frankfurt, while the *Süddeutsche Zeitung* comes from Munich. The German TV networks are also regionally based.

One consequence of decentralization is that Germany's Länder and cities are very consciously in competition with each other for skilled manpower and investment. Germany is a mobile society, geographically as well as socially, and it is easy enough to move from one city or Land to another. This is beginning to modify old differences. Questioning Germans, I found that quite often they had originally come from elsewhere – the older ones from former Eastern territories like Silesia or East Prussia, the younger ones from other Western cities or towns. According to the polls, swinging (though expensive) Munich is the city to which most Germans would like to move.

In the 1990s, the Länder and the cities compete culturally and environmentally as well as economically. Culture and environment are important factors in location decisions by both companies and individuals. *The Economist* of 21 May 1994 contained an advertising section in which the German Länder set out their respective stalls. They all emphasized their skills base, their educational and research systems, and their modern infrastructures but they did not forget their other attractions. The prospective investor also learnt that Baden-Württemberg 'is a good place to live and work – and a wonderful place to get to know', that Hessen provides its residents with 'a very high quality of life and leisure' and that Hamburg and Schleswig-Holstein offer 'a quality lifestyle'.

This competition between regions and cities is healthy and helps to promote experimentation, choice and growth. In the 1950s and 1960s the Ruhrgebiet, with its traditional coal and steel industries, was the powerhouse of the German 'economic miracle'. Then, in the recessionary years of the 1970s and with a shift in demand and technology, Bavaria and Baden-Württemberg made themselves the new centres of expansion. Between 1970 and 1986 economic growth in these two Länder was 40 per cent greater than in North Rhine-Westphalia, Hamburg or Bremen. In addition to BMW and aerospace companies like Dasa, famous names in electronics such as Siemens, Motorola, Hitachi and Texas Instruments have prospered in Bavaria. Baden-Württemberg is home to Daimler-Benz, Bosch and Porsche as well as to IBM, which has its main European plant in Stuttgart. A large number of small and medium-sized firms have also been a characteristic of its economy. So striking was the growth of the two southern Länder in the 1980s that North Rhine-Westphalia and other northern Länder such as Hamburg and Bremen decided that they could learn from their success. North Rhine-Westphalia cleaned up the Ruhr, established new universities and scientific research institutes and encouraged small high-tech firms. In 1994, I saw for myself the change in the Ruhrgebiet – no longer industrial dereliction and pollution but clean rivers and green woods and forests. Though the Ruhr remains Europe's leading industrial area, the economy of the region has become far more diversified and better equipped to survive in the 1990s. So in these ways, the competition between the Länder for new investment and skilled man-power contributes to innovation, renewal and thus the overall success of Germany's economy.

The effectiveness of the federal system, however, depends as much on consensus as on competition – consensus between the different Länder and central Government and between the Länder themselves. The extent of shared powers and the Länder's responsibility for policing and administration means that there has to be a considerable amount of consultation and co-operation. Hardly a day goes by in Bonn without a meeting between Government and Länder officials or ministers.

As described earlier, at national level, the Bundesrat is part of the federal power structure. A potential conflict is created if, as happened in the 1990s, the Bundesrat has a different majority from that in the Bundestag. But the SPD, which is either in power or shares power in all the Länder, except Bavaria and Saxony, has understood that this power has to be used cautiously and constructively if a crippling stalemate is to be avoided. In 1994, a CDU Government minister admitted that 'with different majorities in the Bundestag and the Bundesrat, we already have a *de facto* grand coalition.' The 'different majorities' position illustrates another point about federalism. As Hans-Jochen Vogel, former leader of the SPD, pointed out to me, 'In a federal system, nobody is ever out of power.' Even if a party is in opposition in the Bundestag, it can be in government at Land level or, through its control of the Bundesrat, have a share in power at national level. This involvement reinforces consensus.

The reconstitution of the eastern Länder may have ensured a speedy unification and provided a new form of identity and loyalty. But unification and recession between them have put strains on the federal system and exposed weaknesses.

The need to provide extra resources for the new Länder has threatened to undermine the system of equalizing tax revenue between Länder. Tax revenues, which are nearly all raised by the Federal Government, are mostly shared between the centre and the Länder. The Government and Länder get the majority of their funds from the 'shared taxes', income and corporation tax and VAT. Since some Länder are richer and so derive more from local taxes, the

Equalization Law (*Länderfinanzausgleich*) lays down a redistribution between them so as to ensure that no Land ends up with a tax revenue more than 5 per cent above or below the federal average. But in 1990 equalization was suspended as it applied to the Eastern Länder because, given the poverty of the new Länder, it would have put too great a burden on the Western Länder. Instead a 'German Unity Fund' was set up, financed mainly by federal money and by borrowing.

One of the features of the so-called 'solidarity pact' of March 1993 (see p. 50) was an agreement between the Federal Government and the prime ministers of the sixteen Länder on a relaunching of the equalization arrangements, so that they would apply to the Eastern Länder in 1995. The key to this agreement was giving the Länder a bigger share of VAT, up from 37 per cent to 44 per cent. This provided the Western Länder with an extra DM 20 billion from which to pay for transfers to the Eastern Länder. The question remains, however, whether the increase will prove adequate to help finance the East and whether the tax revenue system will survive in its present form.

The lengthy negotiations over Länder finances highlighted one of the major weaknesses of the federal structure. Progress and reform can only come if there is unanimous agreement, not only between central Government and the Länder but between the Länder themselves. There is already a long agenda of issues which need to be tackled but on which there is no general agreement. These include better co-ordination between social security and unemployment benefits, schools and university reform and improved arrangements for the media.

There are few in Germany who want to go back to a more centralized system of government. The federal structure is, in any case, one part of the constitution which cannot be changed. But there may have to be modifications in the so far highly successful federal system if it is to prove as effective in the future. One suggestion is to allow Länder more independent local tax-raising powers and more autonomy in areas of policy such as education. This would allow a Land more flexibility to initiate change. Arguably, there should also be more 'framework' laws at federal level to set and maintain overall standards.

The debate in the Bundestag in June 1991 over where the seat of government of the newly united country was to be – in Bonn or in Berlin – was a dramatic one. The motion before the Bundestag, that parliament should move to Berlin, was narrowly carried by seventeen votes. The debate raised fundamental questions about the present and future of Germany. Linked to it was the issue of federalism – whether having a bigger and more powerful capital would undermine the federal system.

When Bonn was chosen as the capital of West Germany in 1949, it was made clear that the decision was only provisional, in anticipation of the day when Germany would be united again and Berlin would resume its historic position as the national capital. Bonn was selected because of its relative insignificance. It could not be a city either in the north or the south, because of the opposition which Hamburg would arouse in Munich and vice versa. As a city roughly in the middle, Frankfurt was a serious runner but was considered too important to be only a provisional choice. The clinching voice was that of Konrad Adenauer, Chancellor of the newly formed Federal Republic, who liked Bonn because it was near his native Cologne and because it satisfied his requirement that the new German capital must be 'situated among vineyards, not among potato fields'[6], in other words, as far to the west and as close to France as possible.

In the Bundestag debate, the provisional choice of over forty years earlier proved to have won considerable support. The question at issue was not the title – that was Berlin's by right of the Unity Treaty – but where political decision making should be. Many members spoke up in favour of Bonn because it was the capital of a democratic Germany. As Peter Glotz, a Social Democrat and himself a former Berlin Senator, put it, 'Bonn is the symbol of a new beginning, a necessarily unpretentious, sometimes pitiful new beginning out of the rubble.'[7] Voting for Bonn was a vote for a successful present – and, in the case of civil servants, for, understandably, staying comfortably put rather than moving not just their work but their lives eastwards. 'Just think of the expense' was how the bureaucrats expressed their opposition.

Voting for Bonn was also, as Glotz admitted, a vote against Berlin. In the view of many MPs, Berlin had a bad track record. A German, writing from Düsseldorf to the *Financial Times* in July 1990, summed it up well: 'Berlin has been our capital three times: during the Reich of Bismarck which ended with Versailles; during the Weimar Republic, which ended with Hitler; and during the Nazi period, which ended in disaster and dismemberment.'[8] Another argument against Berlin was that it would weaken federalism. All the Länder governments, except Berlin itself and some in the East, were opposed to Berlin because it could increase centralism and disrupt the balance between the Federal Government and the Länder. However, the ground was cut from under their feet when twelve of their parliaments voted in favour of Berlin. Berlin eventually carried the day because the biggest guns were on its side. The highly respected President, Richard von Weizsäcker, had come out very quickly for the city. Chancellor Kohl, as a Rhinelander, was more cautious but in the end spoke decisively in favour. And Willy Brandt, former Chancellor and Mayor of Berlin when the Wall went up in 1961, was also a powerful advocate.

I like Bonn. John Le Carré rubbished it in *A Small Town in Germany* as 'half as big as the central cemetery in Chicago but twice as dead', while its German disparagers call it *'das Bundesdorf'* (or 'the federal village'). It has many unlovely ministerial buildings and offices, some of them only recently built. And the locals complain about the enervating climate. All the same, it has a splendid market square and a pink rococo Rathaus, a baroque Schloss, formerly the seat of the Archbishop-Electors of Cologne and now used by Bonn university, and some fine nineteenth-century villas, especially towards Bad Godesberg. It also has wonderful views of the Rhine and the Siebengebirge (Seven Mountains), of which the Drachenfels is the most spectacular. It still has the feel of a modest, charming university town rather than a capital city. In its lack of pretension lies its charm.

By contrast, the past weighs heavily on Berlin. There are the militaristic symbols of the Imperial Reich at the Siegessäule, the victory column erected to celebrate the defeat of France in 1870; there are the remains of Hitler's bunker and Göring's Air Ministry, used by the Treuhand as its headquarters; and there are the drab GDR buildings – the party headquarters, the foreign ministry and the Volkskammer building. On a recent tour of Berlin, I felt oppressed by these relics of recent German history – the trophies of the Reich, the legacy of Hitler, the bureaucratic authoritarianism of the GDR – all those buildings which have seen so much strife, violence and human suffering. I wondered whether united Germany, with Berlin as its capital, would be able to put aside the past.

Yet, there is another, more favourable interpretation of the city's history, persuasively argued by Willy Brandt and Richard von Weizsäcker. Since the Berlin airlift of 1948–

49, Berlin has been the symbol of freedom. It is also famous for its culture, its workers' movements, including the East Berlin uprising of 1953, and its brave leaders, like Ernst Reuter and Willy Brandt himself. Bonn was a suitable capital for a divided Germany. Only Berlin can be the capital and the place of government of a united Germany, as well as bringing investment to the East.

For the next decade, Berlin will be the biggest building site in Europe. The designers of the new Berlin have a magnificent opportunity. As I saw for myself, there is plenty of space in the wide central area on either side of the old Wall (now mostly pulled down) and around the Reichstag. But with the opportunity also comes responsibility. The heart of the divided capital, with its Chancellery and ministries, offices and shops, has to be built in a way which is both impressive, yet consistent with Germany's role as a modern democracy. 'Having got rid of the Hohenzollerns, Hitler and Honecker, Berliners don't want any architectural horrors imposed on them,' is the wise conclusion of the city's latest biographers.[9]

The advent of Berlin as Germany's new capital will shift political decision making to the centre of Europe. Bonn is near France, Berlin on the borders of Poland. Yet the absorption of the GDR and the collapse of the Soviet empire made such a move almost inevitable. Unification moved Germany eastwards. As to Berlin's impact on Germany's federal system, there is unlikely to be significant change. The decentralization of Germany has gone too far in constitutional, political and socio-economic terms for a new capital, especially one as relatively small as Berlin, to make any real difference. The government in Berlin will have no greater statutory functions than it had in Bonn, the Länder will retain their powers, and the major cities their attraction. Federalism will remain the guarantee of German liberties. The comment of Björn Engholm, the former leader of the SPD and prime minister of Schleswig-Holstein, is apposite:

> The diversity of initiatives, ideas, productivities, landscapes – this produces an unbelievably diverse, strong Germany, highly differentiated in its internal structure. A Germany which at the same time, because of its federal structure, is not a country which is able once again to overwhelm other nations on the basis of its political power.[10]

## Chapter Five

## FATHERS OF THE REPUBLIC

'One can only say that the Federal Republic has been
fortunate indeed in its rulers, all men of intelligence,
understanding and dedication to duty.'

*Terence Prittie in* The Velvet Chancellors[1]

The drafters of the 1949 'Basic Law', the Federal Republic's
constitution, gave a special position to the Chancellor
because, learning the lesson of Weimar, they believed that
strong parliamentary leadership would be required to
ensure that the new system worked effectively and to give
the regime popular legitimacy.[2] Fortunately, in marked
contrast to the feebleness of most of the politicians of the
Weimar Republic, the Federal Republic has been blessed
with a number of impressive Chancellors. Indeed, taken
as a group, they constitute probably the ablest post-war
leadership of any European nation.

### Adenauer (1949–63) – the old man of the Rhine

Konrad Adenauer became the first Chancellor of the Federal Republic at an age when most politicians have long
since been in retirement. He was seventy-three in 1949, and
told a meeting of CDU notables that he expected to carry
on for two years. In fact, he remained in office for fourteen
years, only leaving, somewhat unwillingly, when he was
eighty-seven.

Adenauer was very much a man of the nineteenth
century, who was already in his thirties when the First
World War broke out. A middle-class conservative, he was
a Catholic Rhinelander who looked naturally towards

France and the West. He hated the Prussian East and, in the 1920s, whenever he had to go to Berlin by train he always drew the curtains at Magdeburg, 'so that I did not have to see the steppes of Asia.'[3] He had a distinguished political career during the Weimar Republic, when he was *Oberbürgermeister* of Cologne and President of the Prussian State Council. In 1926, he was offered the Chancellorship by the Catholic Centre Party but turned it down because he could not be guaranteed a parliamentary majority in the Reichstag. On Hitler's coming to power in 1933, he was sacked as mayor for refusing to allow Nazi flags to be flown on Cologne's principal bridge in Hitler's honour. Though imprisoned twice and sometimes forced to go into hiding, he managed to survive the Third Reich by quietly living in seclusion with his family at his home near Bonn.

In March 1945, the victorious Americans immediately invited Adenauer to become mayor of Cologne again. In October, however, he was dismissed by the British occupying forces because he not only refused to cut down trees in the city park for firewood but insisted that they should provide more coal and building materials. According to his own account, Adenauer was brought into the office of the brigadier in charge of the military government, refused a chair, and curtly informed that he had been sacked. But, instead of retiring for good, Adenauer belatedly launched himself on a national political career as chairman of the newly formed CDU. When the CDU unexpectedly and narrowly won the 1949 election, he was elected Chancellor at the first meeting of the Bundestag by one vote – his own. 'When I was later asked whether I had voted for myself, I replied, "Naturally, anything else would have been hypocrisy."'

Adenauer proved to be an exceptional Chancellor. Golo Mann, the distinguished German historian, once called him a cunning idealist. He was only too well aware of the frailties of his fellow countrymen. Speaking in Luxembourg after the war, he said, 'During the years of National Socialism the Germans behaved so as to make me despise them,' though he added, 'but since 1945 I have learnt to respect my people again.'[4] All the same, he was taking no chances. Although he was prepared to employ civil servants who had been Nazis (provided they repented), he ruled his Cabinet with a rod of iron – he once called himself 70 per cent of the Cabinet – and dominated the Bundestag by force of personality. One shrewd judgement of Adenauer was that he

> was the first German statesman who was able to overcome the unconscious tendency of his countrymen to believe that leaders could only be taken seriously when they wore uniforms. His political style, which was stern, earnest and patriarchal, convinced them that the authority for which they longed could be found in a democratic government under his leadership.[5]

Ruling through coalition, except after the 1957 elections when the CDU won an overall majority, he successfully built up popular support for the Federal Republic. In addition to respect for Adenauer, a key to his domestic success was the so-called 'economic miracle', associated with his Economic Minister, Ludwig Erhard. The amazingly speedy transformation of a shattered and demoralized West Germany into the most powerful economy in Europe ensured that the Bonn Republic did not have to face the appalling economic and social problems which had helped to destroy Weimar.

Above all, Adenauer attached the Federal Republic firmly to the West. Adenauer's vision was European. It was clear to him that Germany's future (or at least the Western part) lay primarily with Western Europe. He firmly believed that it was only through European co-operation and American involvement in Europe that the Soviets could be kept at bay and peace be ensured. Ade-

nauer's pro-Western policy was also good *Realpolitik*. With
the support of the Western Allies, he believed he could
win back Germany's sovereignty. The price which had to
be paid for this was the abandonment of unification, except
as a pious slogan. But Adenauer did not consider that the
Soviet Union would ever agree to a united Germany –
unless it was under Russian control. In his view, West
Germany had no real choice. As he said to an election
meeting, 'We will not go along with the East, ladies and
gentlemen, and we cannot fall between two stones – not
even the Social Democrats want that – so we must go
along with the West.'[6]

The first milestone on the road to integration with the
West came with the Schuman Plan and the establishment
of the European Coal and Steel Community (ECSC) in
1951. The Schuman Plan was the brainchild of the then
head of the French Planning Commission, Jean Monnet,
whose idea was to pool French and German coal and steel
resources under one supranational authority as the first step
towards European unity. On 9 May 1950, an emissary
from the French Foreign Minister, Robert Schuman, arrived in Bonn to present the Plan in the form of a letter
to the Federal Chancellor. The letter made it clear that the
purpose of establishing common control was not only
economic but also political. 'The solidarity in production
thus established will make it plain that any war between
France and Germany becomes not merely unthinkable, but
actually impossible.'[7] Adenauer immediately realized the
significance of the Plan and there and then gave it his
backing. This was the breakthrough for which he had
been working. It was not just that German participation
in the ECSC solved the problem of the Ruhr, then under an international authority set up by the Allies. Far
more important, it represented a decisive first step in the

Federal Republic's emergence as an accepted European state. In 1957, West Germany strengthened its European credentials by being a founder member of the European Economic Community, set up by the Treaty of Rome. As Adenauer said, 'I am the only German Chancellor in history who has preferred the unity of Europe to unity of the Reich.'[8]

The second milestone was reached in May 1955 when the Federal Republic became the fifteenth member of the North Atlantic Treaty Organization (NATO) and West Germany regained its formal sovereignty. At the time, NATO was a second best for Adenauer. He understood clearly that the Western Allies, faced by the breakdown of relations with the Soviet Union and by the outbreak of war in Korea, would favour German rearmament. But, with his long experience, he was strongly against an autonomous German Army and supported instead the idea of a European Defence Community (EDC) which would establish a joint European military organization.

However, in August 1954 the French National Assembly voted against proceeding with a debate on the EDC – tantamount to rejection. Adenauer was deeply disappointed. In an interview with the London *Times*, he asked, 'Must we now assume that the French do not wish for this understanding between our two countries? . . . If the European idea is now wrecked by the action of France, will not that mean a return in Germany to an exaggerated nationalism?'[9] The British got the point. The British Foreign Minister, Anthony Eden, backed by the Americans, offered Germany membership of NATO and of an enlarged Brussels Treaty (signed in 1948 between Britain, France and the Benelux countries) to be called Western European Union. There was to be an independent German national army but its twelve divisions were to be placed at the disposal of the supreme commander of NATO and it was also stipulated that the Federal Republic must not possess nuclear weapons. At the same time, Allied occupation would end and West Germany would become a sovereign state.

Under strong Anglo-American pressure, the French Government and parliament agreed to this new package. Inside Germany there was considerable opposition to a German Army under the slogan *'ohne mich'* (without me). But Adenauer and his coalition accepted the deal because it was the best on offer and because membership of NATO had the merit of locking German military forces into an alliance structure. On 5 May 1955, the Federal Republic became sovereign and, on 9 May, it joined NATO. Speaking in front of the Palais Schaumburg, the Chancellor's official residence, on 5 May, Adenauer read out the Government's proclamation:

> It is with satisfaction that the Federal Government is able to declare: we are once more a free and independent state . . . a free nation ourselves, we are taking our place among the free nations of the world, bound to the former occupation powers in genuine partnership.[10]

His tenacious and consistent strategy had paid off. Seldom in history had a defeated nation been so speedily rehabilitated.

The third milestone – and to Adenauer perhaps his crowning achievement – was the signing of the Franco-German Treaty of Friendship in January 1963. The relationship between Adenauer and de Gaulle is a fascinating one. On the face of it, there were profound differences between these two old men. Adenauer was a convinced European, de Gaulle an unbending French nationalist. Yet they came from the same generation – the generation which had seen two world wars – and both lived in the heartland of Charlemagne's empire, over which France and Germany had fought so fiercely in the recent past. A few months after coming to power in 1958, de Gaulle invited Adenauer to his home at Colombey-les-deux-Églises. By his own account, Adenauer was charmed by his visit, the first made to de Gaulle's private home by a foreign statesman. Certainly, from this first meeting developed a close entente between Bonn and Paris.

From the British point of view, this Franco-German rapprochement had unfortunate immediate consequences. For Adenauer, against the view of most of his Cabinet, backed de Gaulle's veto in January 1963 of the British application to join the European Economic Community. But, even so, the formal ending of nearly a hundred years of rivalry and the establishment of a new Franco-German relationship was of vital importance for the future of the Community. Both countries gained. France, supported by Germany, was able to assume the leading role in Europe, while Germany, working with France, became part of Europe's leadership.

Adenauer clung on to power too long. I remember television shots and newspaper photographs at the beginning of the 1960s of '*der Alte*' with his frail appearance, parchment-like skin and obsidian eyes sunk deep into his almost Asiatic face, seemingly a relic of another age. Maliciously, he played members of his Cabinet against each other and conducted an overt campaign of vilification against Erhard. In the 1959 Presidential crisis, when he first tried to make Erhard accept the presidency, then decided to take it himself (though he later decided against it), Adenauer showed his worst side. He actually told Globke, his head of Chancellery, to research the powers of President to see how the office, under the Basic Law a mainly representative one, could be transformed to allow him continued supremacy. One poll showed that 94 per cent of the country was against him. In the *Der Spiegel* affair of October 1962, Adenauer gave his backing to his Defence

Minister, Franz Josef Strauss, when he illegally instigated a raid on the paper's offices and engineered the arrest of eleven of its staff on the grounds of leaking defence secrets. This fiasco was the final straw and the Chancellor was forced to resign the following year.

Churchill once called Adenauer the greatest German statesman since Bismarck. One of his chief political opponents and a successor as Chancellor, Willy Brandt, summed up his career as follows:

> He made the free part of Germany an ally of the West, lent powerful impulses to West European unity . . . devoted himself to Franco-German reconciliation . . . Even his political opponents of yesterday are conscious that Germany is poorer for the loss of a man who set standards.[11]

Terence Prittie concluded:

> He conquered the despair of Hitler's criminal war, and after the old Germany ceased to exist, he was the principal architect of the new. His was a mighty achievement.[12]

That is a fair assessment.

### Erhard (1963–66) – apostle of the social market

Ludwig Erhard's greatest contribution to the success of the Federal Republic came not as Chancellor but first as Economics Director of the joint Anglo-American Zone and then as Adenauer's Economics Minister. His reassuringly plump figure, his habitual cigar, his ability to explain complicated economic problems simply, and, above all, the success of his policies made him increasingly popular. As Helmut Kohl said of him, 'His name is synonymous with economic recovery after an unparalleled catastrophe. After and alongside Konrad Adenauer he was the most important figure in the young Federal Republic of Germany.'[13]

Erhard once said that, if he had not been born a German, he would have liked to have been an American. Appropriately enough it was the Americans who launched him on a political career. A Bavarian, his refusal to join the Nazi party or even to 'Heil Hitler' had cost him the chance of a professorship. However, his views on the reconstruction of the German economy after a Nazi collapse fell into the hands of the Americans, who appointed him as Bavarian Economics Minister. In March 1948 he became Economics Director of the joint Anglo-American Zone and made his reputation by insisting, against British advice, on ending rationing and price controls at the same time as the D-Mark was introduced. For him it was a political as well as an economic issue. As he said in a radio broadcast, 'Only when every German can freely choose what work he will do and can freely decide what goods he will consume will our people be able to play an active role in the political life of their country.'[14] After initial difficulties, Erhard's gamble came off. By the summer of 1949, output had doubled and there were goods in the shops. When Adenauer became Chancellor, Erhard was the obvious choice as Economics Minister.

His guiding economic philosophy was the very German idea of *Soziale Marktwirtschaft* (or the social market economy), based on free competition but with the support of an extensive welfare system and co-determination between employers and employees. He believed that the most effective way of releasing the energies and skills of the Germans was by abolishing controls and encouraging the market. On the other hand, Erhard's capitalism had a strong social dimension. Influenced by Catholic social teachings, he was insistent on the need for consensus in industry and for protection of the weakest members of society. 'Prosperity for all' was his watchword.

Erhard has been called the father of the *Wirtschaftswunder*.

It would perhaps be more accurate to call him its 'enabler'. He certainly followed steady and consistent policies. But Erhard himself said in 1954,

> That which has taken place in Germany these past years was anything other than a miracle. It was merely the result of honest endeavour of a whole people, who again had the chance of applying human initiative, human liberty and human energies.[15]

There were other factors. Export-led growth was due to the combination of an undervalued D-Mark, a plentiful labour supply (two-and-a-half million people left East for West Germany between 1949 and 1961), good industrial relations, a well trained labour force and sustained industrial investment, and the psychological as well as the economic spur provided by the Marshall Plan, followed by the outbreak of the Korean war in 1950. The coming of the Common Market gave an added boost. During the 1950s and 1960s, the German growth rate was the fastest in Europe and living standards trebled. No wonder that Erhard was so popular, that the CDU won elections, and that the Germans supported the Federal Republic.

When Erhard at last succeeded Adenauer as Chancellor in 1963, he proved to be a disappointment. He was strongly pro-American, less enthusiastic about de Gaulle than Adenauer and made some tentative steps towards improving relations with the East. He won the 1965 Federal Election, in part because of his personal prestige. But he found it difficult to control his party and almost impossible to cope with his predecessor, Adenauer, whom he foolishly allowed to continue as party chairman. A typically contemptuous Adenauer comment came in response to a suggestion that there was no government under Erhard: 'That is quite wrong,' said Adenauer. 'There are at least three governments and he is not in charge of any of them.' When in 1966 there was a slackening in the rate of growth and controversy over how to pay for Government spending, his coalition partners, the FDP, deserted him and forced his resignation. It was Willy Brandt who pointed out that 'It was ironical that Ludwig Erhard should have foundered on the very rock, that of economics, whose avoidance had earned him such acclaim as a successful helmsman.'[16] All the same, he had made a vital contribution to German democracy.

## Willy Brandt (1969–74) – man of integrity

As Willy Brandt became the first Social Democrat and fourth Chancellor of the Federal Republic in October 1969, he said that now Hitler had lost the war and that he considered himself Chancellor not of a conquered but of a liberated Germany. For me, as for millions of Europeans, the election of Brandt was the sign that Germany really had changed. As Chancellor, he had great achievements, both domestic and foreign, to his credit. But over and above that he brought to European politics a unique integrity and moral stature. When the novelist Günter Grass was asked why he was campaigning for Brandt's victory in the 1969 election, he replied: 'Because Brandt will shorten the legs of lies.'[17]

For many of us, Brandt was a political hero. I only met him twice, though I listened to a number of his speeches. Though not much taller than medium height, he had a great presence, partly because of his erect carriage. He had one of those open, north German faces and a warm smile, which was devastating to women. His voice was deep and rasping (probably because of his smoking habit). He was often an inspiring speaker, though his language could be somewhat cloudy and imprecise. The last time I heard him was at a meeting of European Socialists in the old Reichstag building in Berlin in February 1990. The grand old man of

Social Democracy was in tremendous form, heralding German unification and the triumph of democracy in Eastern Europe but warning us of the dangers of nationalism. He spoke movingly about the need for European unity. He died in October 1992.

As Heinrich Böll wrote, Brandt's career was 'a legend, almost a fairy tale which came true'.[18] Born as Herbert Frahm in 1913 in Lübeck, he was an illegitimate son of a poor salesgirl and was brought up by his grandfather, a truck driver and committed SPD member. In the dying days of Weimar, an impatient young Brandt left the SPD because of its ineffectiveness and joined the left-wing Socialist Workers Party (SAP). When the Nazis came to power, he escaped arrest by fleeing to Norway (he became a Norwegian citizen) and then, when Norway was invaded, to Sweden. In exile, he worked closely with the German underground, including making a clandestine trip to Berlin in 1936. In 1944, he was sent a message by Julius Leber, SPD leader and one of the July 1944 conspirators, to ask him to work with a new German Government if and when Hitler was eliminated. After the war he covered the Nuremberg trials as a journalist and then went to Berlin as Norwegian press attaché. It was not until 1948 that he became a German citizen again, legally taking the name of Willy Brandt, which he had used as a disguise in 1933. Brandt's first great contribution to West Germany came through his work in Berlin. He was right-hand man of Ernst Reuter, the governing mayor of West Berlin, during the 1948–49 Soviet blockade when the Berliners astonished the world with their courage and endurance. In 1957, he became mayor himself and was at the helm when the Wall was erected in August 1961. He was on an election special train at Hanover as SPD candidate in the Federal Election that year when he received an urgent message asking him to return to Berlin at once. He went back to find the same

scene everywhere, 'Construction workers, roadblocks, concrete posts, barbed wire, GDR soldiers.'[19] Brandt calmed
and encouraged West Berliners but he was deeply disappointed by the lack of Western response. President
Kennedy did not even interrupt his yachting holiday.
This was a crucial moment for Brandt. As he wrote
later,

> Ulbricht had been allowed to take a swipe at the Western
> superpower, and the United States merely winced with annoy-
> ance. My political deliberations in the years that followed were
> substantially influenced by this day's experience, and it was
> against this background the so-called *Ostpolitik* – the beginning
> of détente – took shape.[20]

In short, what happened – and did not happen – in Berlin
in 1961 was the key to Brandt's policy towards the East, as
pursued both by the grand coalition (whose Chancellor
was the CDU's Kurt-Georg Kiesinger) when he was
Foreign Minister and under the SPD-FDP Governments
which he led.

Brandt saw *Ostpolitik* as a complement to Adenauer's
Western policy. As he conceived it, it drew its strength
from the Federal Republic's Western alliances and needed
the support of West Germany's partners. He described his
Eastern policy as follows – improved relations with the
Soviet Union, normal relations with the East European
states and a *modus vivendi* between the two parts of Germany. He achieved these objectives remarkably quickly.
Treaties were signed with the Soviet Union, Poland and
lastly with the GDR. A four-power agreement was also
struck over Berlin, guaranteeing its communications. His
policy has been criticized on the grounds that, by accepting
the division of Europe, *Ostpolitik* delayed rather than has-
tened the collapse of the Soviet Empire and the unification
of Germany. But, according to Brandt, its purpose was
precisely to initiate change:

Above and beyond the German question, we felt it impossible to persevere in a simple acceptance of prevailing conditions in Europe. What really mattered was to create a climate in which the *status quo* could be changed – in other words, improved – by peaceful means. I was unjustly accused . . . of bowing to realities. I was, and still am, of the opinion that realities can be influenced for the better.[21]

In other words, he was accepting the *status quo* in order to try to change it. And, given what happened in 1989–90, it is difficult to argue that, in the longer term, the overall aim of the policy was unsuccessful. My view is that he thoroughly deserved the Nobel Peace Prize which he won in 1971. Brandt wanted to be not only a 'foreign policy' Chancellor but also a *Kanzler der inneren Reformen* (Chancellor of domestic reform). He believed that the SPD election successes in 1969 and in 1972, when for the first time the SPD won more votes than the CDU-CSU, gave him a mandate for change. Rejecting the Adenauer formula of '*Keine Experimente*', he said, 'Don't be afraid of experiments, let us create a modern Germany,' and, 'If we want to live in security tomorrow, we must fight for reform today.' The Brandt governments introduced a number of social improvements, including the extension of pension rights, the provision of sick pay for employees and an expanded health insurance scheme. They widened educational opportunity considerably, so much so that the chances of a twenty-year-old working-class child born in 1958 reaching a university or college were approximately six times greater than they had been for a similar child born in 1948.[22] And they also strengthened Germany's consensus industrial relations system by extending co-determination at factory level. At their 1959 Bad Godesberg conference, the SPD had accepted the principles of Erhard's 'social market'. In power, Brandt showed the Germans that not only was it possible to strengthen the social side of the 'social market' without undermining the economy but also that social reform was essential if the fruits of growth were to be more widely shared.

In May 1974, Brandt dramatically resigned when it was revealed that one of his advisers in the Federal Chancellery was an East German spy. Though his Finance Minister, Helmut Schmidt, urged him not to resign, he felt that he had to take personal responsibility. In his memoirs, he also admitted that he was facing increasing difficulties 'in and with his government which weakened his will to fight'.[23] He was presumably referring to the 1973 oil price hike and to criticisms made by Schmidt, by the SPD floor leader, Herbert Wehner, and by the FDP as to the way Brandt was running his Government and party. But a writer in the *New York Times* rightly pointed out that it was impossible to imagine any of his predecessors acting in the same way and that historians might well conclude that Brandt's most durable achievement lay not in foreign but in domestic policy because he had 'institutionalized the practice of democracy in a nation with limited democratic experience.'[24]

For many of us, the abiding memory of Brandt will be the image of him kneeling at the Warsaw ghetto memorial, deeply moved by the occasion. One journalist wrote, 'Then he who does not need to kneel knelt on behalf of all who ought to kneel, but do not because they dare not, or cannot.'[25] It revealed the great humanity and humility of the man – and did a power of good for the reputation of the Germans. As Denis Healey put it, 'This spontaneous gesture of penitence was worth a million speeches.'[26] It was the defining moment of Brandt's career.

*Helmut Schmidt (1974–82) – crisis manager*

Helmut Schmidt was very different from Willy Brandt – a

pragmatist rather than an idealist, a crisis manager rather than a conciliator, very much the professional who brought unmatched political and administrative experience and skill to the Chancellorship. As Chancellor, he called himself the Federal Republic's 'senior executive'. In many ways, he was the best man for the recessionary years of the 1970s and early 1980s.

During my early years in Parliament, Schmidt was Europe's outstanding leader. I first heard him speak at the December 1974 Labour Party conference. Threats had been made by some of Labour's anti-Europeans that they would walk out if Schmidt's speech was too aggressively propagandistic. Schmidt disarmed them by saying that he felt like someone trying to convince the Salvation Army of the virtues of drink. The decision about Europe was one for the delegates but, in the name of solidarity, he would like them to know that Labour's comrades on the Continent wanted them to stay in – in Continental interests as much as in Britain's. It was a bravura performance made in flawless English which had all but the most churlish of anti-marketeers on their feet.

Later in the 1980s, I met him several times at Königswinter conferences. Physically, he was quite small, though with a fine head and piercing grey eyes. He was formidably intelligent, always lucid and extremely abrasive with anyone who he thought was wasting his time or speaking foolishly. In 1980 I observed him grimacing when Mrs Thatcher spent much of a speech she made at a dinner given by her for the Federal Chancellor at Cambridge upbraiding the Germans about the British financial contribution to the EC. A few years later, after he had left office, I heard him say that, though a convinced Anglophile, perhaps de Gaulle had been right after all when he vetoed British entry. His hopes about Britain had been dashed. He once told the distinguished British journalist, the late Peter

Jenkins, that Britain was 'an underdeveloped country'. I came to understand why he was called '*Schmidt Schnauze*' (Schmidt the lip).

Son of a teacher, Schmidt was born in Hamburg in 1918, which made him five years younger than Brandt and a member of the 'generation between generations', too young to be politically aware in the years leading to Nazi rule but old enough to go to war in 1939. He joined the Hitler Youth in 1934 when his rowing club was assimilated by the Nazi organization but was suspended for being in favour of the German Expressionist school of painting. Schmidt said of his upbringing that he was influenced 'atmospherically by his father against the Third Reich but not in favour of anything else' and that he 'had no concrete impression of what a democracy looked like'.[27] His family's cautious attitude may have been affected by the fact that his grandfather was a Jew. After two years conscription, he was called up when the war came and in 1941 was posted as an officer to the Russian front where he won the Iron Cross. Transferred back to Berlin, it became clear to him that this was a 'criminal government', though he carried on, despite inner conflict. In a speech at a Cologne syna-gogue in 1978, Schmidt said of German behaviour under the Nazis that 'the truth is that most people, faint at heart, kept their silence'.

In the summer of 1945, he was made a prisoner of war and it was in a prisoner of war camp that he decided to join the SPD. Hence the jibe, 'Helmut Schmidt learned his socialism in the officers' mess.' After studying economics at Hamburg University, he worked as an economist and administrator for the Hamburg Land Government and was elected to the Bundestag in 1953 as an SPD MP. Returning to Hamburg as Minister of Internal Affairs, he first made his reputation as a crisis manager, when his leadership saved thousands of lives after the Elbe burst its banks in

February 1962. When the Grand Coalition was formed, Schmidt became SPD floor leader. Under the Brandt Governments, Schmidt was first Defence Minister, later for a short time 'Superminister' of Economics and Finance and then Minister of Finance. He was the obvious choice to lead the SPD–FDP coalition when Brandt resigned.

Schmidt was the 'recession' Chancellor who guided the Federal Republic through the difficult times. Under him, the German economy recovered quicker from the 1973 oil shock than did others. At the same time, the Schmidt Government managed to preserve the social gains of the Brandt years. Schmidt campaigned in the 1976 election, which the centre left coalition narrowly won, on the slogan *Modell Deutschland*, emphasizing not only Germany's superior economic record but also showing how this was linked to the social cohesion which Schmidt and his ministers worked so hard to sustain. He said:

> Our country owes our high position to our successful policy of rapprochement, to our exceptionally high economic capacity, to our tightly knit system of social security, to our policy of constant reforms – and to the fact that we have put into practice our intentions about promoting social solidarity and real freedom for the individual.

In other words, from being a pariah nation after the war, the Federal Republic had become a model democratic society to which both West and East Europeans looked with respect. Schmidt did not exaggerate. In the 1970s and early 1980s many of us in the British Labour Party were greatly impressed by German achievements. I also remember being told by a Polish Communist leader in 1980 that young Poles looked not to the Soviet Union or even to the United States but to Schmidt's Germany.

One of the challenges which the Federal Republic had to face in the 1970s was terrorism. There had already been the horrific 1972 Munich Olympic Games massacre when

members of the Israeli team had been murdered by the
PLO, as well as a number of assassinations by the radical
middle-class German group, the Baader-Meinhof gang.
In September 1977, the President of the German Employers Association, Hanns-Martin Schleyer, was kidnapped
by the Red Army Faction but Schmidt refused to give
way to their ultimatum that eleven prisoners, including
Andreas Baader, Ulrike Meinhof and Gudrun Ensslin,
should be set free. To make things even more difficult,
in October four Arab terrorists hijacked a Lufthansa
Boeing with eighty-six passengers on board, forced the
plane to land at Mogadishu in Somalia, and demanded
the freeing of these prisoners. Schmidt masterminded a
brilliant rescue operation carried out by a German special
unit formed after Munich. Within hours, Baader, Meinhof and Ensslin committed suicide and Hanns-Martin Schleyer was murdered. On hearing of the successful operation, Schmidt broke down and wept with relief, though
he was deeply upset by the news two nights later that
Schleyer had been found dead in the boot of an abandoned car. If the Mogadishu rescue operation had gone
wrong, Schmidt said that he would have resigned. 'No
one would have persuaded me otherwise. I was fully
determined.'

The Schleyer affair was a turning point in the fight
against terrorism. Terrorist incidents decreased dramatically. Although there was much debate about the anti-
terrorist laws introduced by the Government, Schmidt's
decisive leadership had shown that the Federal Republic
could defend itself effectively against extremists – and
West Germany won much credit abroad. As his biographer put it, 'Suddenly there seemed to be something
more to be proud of than a relatively successful economy.
A German force had acted abroad to protect the weak,
not to conquer.'

His period in office coincided with the emergence of the Federal Republic as what one eminent German commentator described as a 'European Great Power'[28]. West Germany was the strategic outpost of the NATO alliance and also the main bridge between East and West Europe. Most important of all was Germany's new economic power, though this strength was relative. The Federal Republic might have done better than her European rivals in the post-oil-shock world, but her GNP was still only a third of that of the USA and smaller than that of Japan. And her dependence on exports meant that she had to be concerned with the economic performance and policies of other countries.

Schmidt never made the mistake of overestimating German power. 'I am speaking on behalf of a country that cannot and will not act as a big power,' he declared to the UN General Assembly in May 1978. As a Social Democrat who had fought in the war, he was chary of independent initiatives, working through alliances and international organizations, through the EC, NATO, the OECD, and the new Western economic Summits, as well as the established partnerships with France, the United States and the United Kingdom and the relations with the Eastern Bloc countries. His relationship with the French President, Valéry Giscard d'Estaing, like Schmidt also a former Finance Minister, was so close, even though they communicated in English, that there was much talk of the 'Helmut and Valéry' show. He also got on well with the British Labour Prime Minister, James Callaghan, and with the Chancellor of the Exchequer, Denis Healey, whom he had known when they were both Defence Ministers. He thought President Carter of the United States was a bungling amateur who failed to understand German concerns about the Soviet build-up of intermediate nuclear missiles in Europe. Even so, in January 1979, Schmidt was invited for the first time to a special summit of top NATO powers – the United States, Britain and France – at Guadeloupe. This was both a recognition of West Germany's enhanced importance and of the strength of Schmidt's arguments for a 'twin track' approach, whereby NATO would match Soviet medium-range missile deployment if necessary but would also be ready not to deploy if the Soviet bloc removed its arsenal.

Schmidt was a creative international statesman. He was the driving force behind the European Monetary System (EMS) set up in 1979 to provide a zone of monetary stability in Europe. The EMS has had its traumas, particularly in September 1992 and August 1993. It is debatable whether it can provide the basis for a single currency, as envisaged in the Maastricht Treaty. But it has lasted over fifteen years and, by and large, fulfilled its objective. He was also an important influence on initiatives for which Giscard got the credit, most notably the European Council and the Western economic summit meetings. And though he left office too soon to see the eventual agreement on medium-range nuclear missiles, his 'twin track' strategy was triumphantly vindicated.

Schmidt defeated Strauss in the 1980 federal elections, but his political position was soon undermined by unrest in his party, especially over the 'twin track' policy; by a new assertiveness by the FDP, which had improved its electoral position in 1980; the impact of the second oil shock; and by his own poor health (he had to have a pacemaker operation in October 1981). When it became obvious that the FDP were preparing to desert the coalition, Schmidt pre-empted their move by sacking the FDP ministers. A CDU/FDP coalition under Kohl was then formed after a constructive vote of no confidence (see p. 104); Schmidt resigned both as Chancellor and parliamentary party leader and the new coalition won the subsequent election comfort ably in March 1983. A shrewd judgement on the Schmidt Chancellorship is provided by his biographer:

> His contribution may be called less 'original' than that of Adenauer and Brandt, but it was no less vital. It was not a foregone conclusion that the young German democracy would cope so well with the shocks of the late 1970s. Schmidt's steady leadership, his clear sighted defence of the middle ground in politics against dreamers and fanatics, helped bring his country stability and won it more respect abroad.

Both as a Briton and a European, I always felt that much safer knowing that Helmut Schmidt was Chancellor of the Federal Republic in such difficult times.

## Helmut Kohl (1982–) – 'unification' Chancellor

Helmut Kohl has been consistently underrated not only by his opponents but even sometimes by his own supporters. His style is pedestrian, his speeches often dull, and he has sometimes made the most embarrassing gaffes, so much so that he has been called 'BlunderKohl'. Yet his achievements are highly impressive. He has won four successive elections and controls his party firmly. He has been a consistent and creative European statesman. Above all, he had the single-mindedness, courage and energy to push through unification with the utmost speed.

The first thing one notices about Kohl is his size. He is built like a well fed front row Rugby forward and, when necessary, uses his height to dominate those around him. I first met Kohl at an official Foreign Office lunch in 1981. I wish I could say that I immediately realized that I was meeting someone who was going to help change the course of history. Still, my lack of foresight was shared by many others. An American State Department official once told me that when he met Kohl, who was then Prime Minister of the Rhineland-Palatinate, he reported back that

Kohl would never make it to national politics. When I next saw Kohl in the year of unification at the Königswinter Conference it was clear that an enormous change had come over him. Self-confidence and authority literally oozed out of him. Beside him, Mrs Thatcher, who was also there, sounded, and indeed was, shrill and narrow-minded. The more I see him in action, the more I realize that the key to his success is his boundless self belief. It has allowed him to come back · from disappointments and setbacks which would have knocked out lesser men. His determination was never more clearly displayed than in the year of 1994, when, after trailing in the polls, he overhauled the SPD to win a narrow victory.

Like Konrad Adenauer, whom he greatly admires, Helmut Kohl is a Rhinelander. He was born at Ludwigs-hafen in the Rhineland-Palatinate in 1930. Too young to take part in the war (though he remembers over 100 bombing raids) he studied at Frankfurt and Heidelberg before joining the Chemical Employers' Association in his home town. A Catholic with strong religious convictions, he joined the CDU when he was sixteen and rose rapidly in his Land party, becoming prime minister in 1969. He was CDU Chancellor candidate in 1976, when he was only narrowly defeated by Helmut Schmidt and, though Franz-Josef Strauss replaced him in 1980, his control of the CDU as party chairman and leader of the CDU-CSU group in the Bundestag meant that he was in an excellent position to stage a comeback when Strauss self-destructed and Schmidt faltered.

In office, Kohl proved that he had a safe pair of hands and was a reliable European and international partner. Domestically, despite talk of a fundamental political change, his Government continued with the Social Market, social consensus policies of previous governments, albeit from a more conservative perspective. There was little of

the radical restructuring and privatization associated with
Mrs Thatcher. He also pursued the same international
policies as his predecessor, for example sticking firmly to
Schmidt's 'twin track' approach and supporting *Ostpolitik*.
He may have been closer to the Americans than Schmidt
(which was to stand him in good stead when unification
came). But he also had, like Schmidt and Adenauer before
him, a firm partnership with the French, though now it
was 'the Helmut and François' show.

His finest hour came over unification. All his instincts –
historical, political, populist – pointed in the same direction
and he went for the main chance with a boldness and a
skill which even some of his closest admirers may not have
known he possessed. Interestingly, his two predecessors,
Schmidt and Brandt, said the decision in favour of a quick
unification was correct, and that Kohl deserves the main
credit. Where he can and should be criticized is for his
failure to tell the Germans about the cost of unification. 'I
waited and waited for the "*Blut, Schweiss und Tränen*"
(Blood, Sweat and Tears) speech and it never came,' said
Helmut Schmidt.[30]

It has been of great benefit to the Federal Republic –
and to Europe – that unification should have come under a
Chancellor who is such a deeply committed European.
Kohl likes to point out that he has advocated both German
unification and European integration ever since he first
became interested in politics as a teenager.[31] His European
track record has been excellent. Together with his close
associate, Jacques Delors, then President of the European
Commission, he has been one of the driving forces in the
most creative burst in the history of European integration
since the early days, including the completion of the internal market, the Single European Act and the Maastricht
Treaty itself. Whatever its imperfections, one of the merits
of the Maastricht Treaty is that it binds Germany closer

than ever before to its partners in the European Union. For that, other Europeans as well as Germans owe a debt of gratitude to Helmut Kohl. He is certainly a clever party politician but he is also a statesman who has had as big an influence on the development of the Federal Republic and Western Europe as any of his illustrious predecessors.

The Federal Republic has been fortunate in having a succession of Chancellors who have lived up to the challenges of their times. Consider the record: Konrad Adenauer established West German democracy on stable foundations and attached it firmly to the United States and Western Europe. Ludwig Erhard was, if not the architect, then certainly the enabler of the *Wirtschaftswunder* (economic miracle). Willy Brandt introduced social reforms, championed reconciliation with Eastern Europe and in his person best symbolized the new democratic Germany to the world. Helmut Schmidt was the cool crisis manager who showed that the Federal Republic was not just a 'fair weather' construct. Helmut Kohl has been the 'unification' Chancellor and consistent supporter of European integration. They are a formidable bunch, and certainly superior to the comparable group of post-war British prime ministers.

## Chapter Six

## DEMOCRATS AND EXTREMISTS

'Weimar was a democracy without democrats: Bonn not only has the support of an overwhelming majority but is also based on firm conviction and strong institutions.'

*Robert Leicht, editor of* Die Zeit

The Weimar Republic was a catastrophic failure. The Bonn Republic has been an outstanding success. Since the establishment of the Federal Republic in 1949, elections have been fair; governments have been stable; liberties have been protected; a wide consensus has been maintained; and democracy has flourished. To its many admirers, it is, a model democratic state. Yet, because of the past, the question that is still asked by pessimistic foreigners and even faint-hearted Germans is how far democracy has really taken root in Germany. Could it survive a big economic or political setback? And to what extent do extremists, especially neo-Nazi groups, pose a real threat? As the 1990 Chequers Memorandum bluntly put it,

While we all admired and indeed envied what the Germans had achieved in the last forty-five years, the fact was that their institutions had not yet been tested by adversity such as a major economic calamity . . . Could some of the unhappy characteristics of the past re-emerge with just as destructive consequences?

The overriding objective of the delegates who drew up the constitution of the Federal Republic – the Basic Law – was to avoid the mistakes of Weimar. This was hardly surprising as many of them had been Weimar politicians, including Konrad Adenauer, soon to be Chancellor, Kurt Schumacher, the leader of the SPD, and Theodor Heuss, later to become President of the new Republic, and they had, therefore, seen at first hand its glaring shortcomings. Although the Basic Law begins with an impressive list of individual freedoms, a leading expert on the German political system points out that it 'reflects a sustained attempt at rectification rather than a desire to construct a visionary democratic order.'[1]

The Weimar Republic faced a number of handicaps which were far more serious than any constitutional weaknesses. It was unfairly blamed for the humiliation of the Versailles Treaty, so that for many 'democracy became synonymous with national humiliation and, increasingly, with economic ruin.'[2] It had to try and deal with the great inflation of 1923 and the Great Depression which began in 1929. And at no stage did it have the support of élites – the business leaders, landowners, military and top civil servants, some of whom helped bring Hitler to power. Indeed, when the crunch came in March 1933, Weimar had no real defenders, except the SPD who, to their credit, were the only party to vote against Hitler's Enabling Law which transferred power from parliament to his Government.

However, when the former Weimar politicians met in Bonn in 1948 to draw up a new constitution, they were determined to avoid what they saw as the constitutional blunders of Weimar – an overstrong President who was independent of the legislature, and the weakness and multiplicity of political parties. Learning the lessons of Hitler, they were also intent on limiting powers of government, through federalism (see Chapter 4) and through the setting up of a Constitutional Court, not only to adjudicate between the centre and the regions but also to protect the basic rights laid down in the Basic Law.

In Bonn democracy the key figure is not the President but the Chancellor (see Chapter 5). Because the Chancellor has to be elected by the Bundestag, the office derives constitutional authority not directly from the voters but from the elected members of the Bundestag. In other words, the Federal Republic is a *parliamentary* rather than a *presidential* democracy. To guard against the 'negative' majorities which made the Weimar parliament unworkable in its later stages, the Bundestag is only able to express its lack of confidence in the Chancellor by electing a successor. This innovative constitutional procedure has only been used twice – in 1972 when the CDU-CSU opposition came within two votes of unseating Willy Brandt by nominating Rainer Barzel to replace him, and in 1982 when the CDU-CSU, with FDP support, removed Helmut Schmidt and replaced him with Helmut Kohl.

A feature of the constitution of the Federal Republic is the special place given to political parties. This was devised partly to safeguard and enhance their position, so as to prevent a repetition of their failure under Weimar, and partly to ensure against the rise of another Nazi party. The Basic Law declares that 'the parties participate in the forming of the political will of the people'. In other words, a key role of the parties is to act as recruiting sergeants of democracy, a service for which they are supported by public money. At the same time, they must publicly account for their funds; their organizations must be democratic; and parties which seek to overturn democracy or endanger the existence of the Federal Republic are unconstitutional (as directed by the Constitutional Court).

Over and above their formal constitutional position, the parties are the lynchpins of the parliamentary democracy established by the Basic Law, so much so that one authority has concluded that 'the Basic Law was written by and for the benefit of the post-war parties.'[3] No Chancellor can govern without their support, and it is with the backing of a political party that a prospective member of the Bundestag seeks the votes of the electorate. Politicians are far more likely to be successful if they are members of either one of the two big parties (the CDU/CSU or the SPD) or one of three smaller parties (the FDP, or the Greens, or, in East Germany, the PDS). This is because, in order to prevent the fragmentation of the party system, the federal electoral system, which combines the Weimar principle of proportionality with the relative majority system of single-member constituencies, as in Britain, has an electoral threshold before a party can qualify for seats in the Bundestag – first 5 per cent in any one Land, then 5 per cent of the federal vote (introduced in 1953) or three constituency seats (since 1957). The first Bundestag had eleven parties, the 1994 one only six. So important are the political parties in the Federal Republic that Bonn has been called a '*Parteienstaat*' (or Party State).

On the Godesberger Allee in Bonn there are two large and ugly modern buildings within two hundred metres of each other – one is the Christian Democratic Union (CDU) headquarters, the other that of the Social Democratic Party (SPD). Here, as much as in the Bundestag, is the heart of political Germany where the democratic makers and shakers came together.

The tallest building is occupied by the CDU, which is arguably the most successful party of the right in Europe. It has been in government for all but eleven years since the Federal Republic was founded and has provided four out of the six Federal Chancellors. The CDU, which was formed after the war, drew on the strengths and traditions of the old Catholic Centre party which had played an important role in imperial and Weimar Germany but, unlike Christian Democratic parties in other European countries, it emerged from an alliance between Catholics and Protestants – both of whom felt their churches had done too little to resist Hitler. There was also an important

strain derived from Catholic teaching about social responsibility which inhibited the CDU from becoming a traditional conservative party. Indeed its 1947 Ahlen programme
went so far as to reject capitalist notions of profit and
power and called for a new structure which would serve
the prosperity of all the people. Though this anti-capitalist
rhetoric was soon discarded by Adenauer and Erhard in
favour of the 'social market', the social dimension has
continued to play a significant role in the party's thinking.

The CDU has been described as the party of the 'double
compromise' – between Catholics and Protestants and between capital and labour.[4] Its Bavarian wing, the CSU,
which preserves its organizational independence while forming, with the CDU, one grouping (*fraktion*) in the Bundestag, also brings its own more rural, regional and right-
wing flavour to the CDU. Together these elements have
provided a potent amalgam which has helped make the
CDU a classic *Volkspartei* or 'catch-all' party able to appeal
across class and sectional boundaries.

Some British Conservative politicians, like Chris Patten
and David Hunt, have spoken of their affinity with the
CDU, while John Major, in the speech to the Konrad
Adenauer *Stiftung* in March 1991, in which he said he
wanted Britain to be 'at the very heart of Europe', claimed
that British Conservative Party philosophy had 'much in
common with the basic tenets of Christian democracy'.
The reality is otherwise. As recent differences over the
European Social Chapter and the future of the European
Union have clearly shown, the CDU, though, like the
Conservatives, deriving support from business and the self-
employed, is far more of a pro-European, social consensus
party than the British Conservatives. Meeting Christian
Democrat politicians at conferences over the last twenty
years, I have been struck by how little they are attracted to
Thatcherite Conservatism. 'Please remember, we are not

Thatcherites,' a CDU member of the Bundestag once begged of me. They are committed to social welfare, support co-determination in industry and consider themselves a post-national party, pledged to European integration.

The CDU has played a vital part in the success of the Federal Republic. It has provided the main party of government, though almost always in coalition, mostly with the Free Democrats but, if necessary, with the SPD. It has been highly effective in mobilizing electoral support, consistently polling between about 44 per cent and 48 per cent of the total vote, though it dropped below 42 per cent in 1994, for the first time. Like the SPD, it is a 'membership party', with a relatively high proportion of members to voters, essential in keeping in touch with the electorate.

Equally important, its massive presence on the right of German politics, combined with the Bundestag electoral threshold, has acted as a so-far insuperable barrier against the rise of a significant extremist or neo-Nazi party at federal level. At the same time, the need to seek votes across class and sectional lines has discouraged the CDU from itself becoming a purely right-wing party. The attempt of Franz Josef Strauss, the CSU leader from Bavaria, to shift the party to the right failed at the 1980 federal elections where the CDU was beaten by the SPD-FDP coalition. If such a 'vacuum cleaner' of a party, always eager to suck in votes to both its right and its left, has sometimes seemed to lack a clear identity, this has often been compensated for by a leader with a strong profile, such as Adenauer or the post-unification Kohl. In recent years, the successful projection of national unity and of economic competence has compensated for a shrinking of the party's natural constituency, as the proportion of churchgoers and farmers in the population declines.[5] Looking ahead, there is every prospect that the CDU will continue to play a pivotal role in politics – to the undoubted benefit of German democracy.

I am more familiar with the SPD than with any other political party except my own. Over thirty years, I have visited it, studied it, written about it and learnt from its example. I have had discussions with Social Democrat members, officials, local councillors and Land and Federal MPs, and occasionally their leaders. I have rejoiced at the party's successes and grieved at its setbacks. Indeed I have always felt so much at home with German Social Democrats that there were times in the early 1980s when I was more at ease with them than with some members of the British Labour Party.

In contrast to the CDU, the SPD has a long and proud history. It is one of the oldest political parties in Europe and the oldest Socialist party. Founded in 1863, it adopted a Marxist programme in 1891, and by 1912 had, with support of the industrial workers, become the largest party in the Imperial Reichstag. The SPD was the main party of the Weimar Republic. Its leader, Friedrich Ebert, was the first President and it provided four of its Chancellors. But its record under Weimar was a patchy one. The Social Democrats failed (though other parties were also to blame) to establish the Republic on a firm basis. When they were in government, their performance was not very impressive. Imprisoned by their own Marxist ideology, they could not provide any kind of answer to the slump. And, although they voted against the Enabling Act, they did not succeed in putting up an effective resistance to Hitler. All the same, unlike most other German politicians, their democratic credentials remained impeccable. Under Hitler, their leaders were either killed or imprisoned in concentration camps, or went into exile, so it was not unreasonable for the Social Democrats, led by the fiery Kurt Schumacher, to expect to dominate the politics of post-war West Germany. Instead, looking increasingly irrelevant, they lost three successive elections and, by the end of the 1950s, seemed condemned to perpetual opposition.

The turning point in the SPD's fortunes came in 1959 when it adopted the Bad Godesberg programme. The new approach, as one of its authors said, was ethical in aim, democratic in method, and pragmatic in policy. It represented an abandonment of Marxism and an acceptance of the social market economy, tempered by an emphasis on the overall economic and social responsibilities of Government. The formula which best sums up the flavour of Bad Godesberg is, 'As much competition as possible – as much planning as necessary.' Electorally, it opened the way for SPD success by widening its appeal beyond its original working-class base. Like the CDU, the SPD became a *Volkspartei*, able to reach out to other social groups in order to create a new centre-left majority. Ten years after Bad Godesberg, Willy Brandt became the first SPD Chancellor of the Federal Republic.

The highpoint of the SPD's fortunes in post-war Germany was from 1969 to 1982, under the Chancellorships of Willy Brandt and Helmut Schmidt, when the party led Germany. In the 1976 federal elections, there was a poster of Schmidt and Brandt strolling through a sunlit park, which summed up for me the SPD at its post-war best. Here were the head and the heart of German Social Democracy, impressive guarantors of the progressive, democratic society that had emerged from the ruins of 1945.

Since 1982, however, the party has been in opposition and sometimes seemed to have lost its way. The changing social structure, the growth of issue-orientated politics and unification itself have put the SPD on the defensive. The strength of the Greens throughout Germany and, to a lesser extent, the repackaging of the former Communist party in the form of the PDS in the eastern Länder has created new competition on the left. On the other hand, the SPD cannot afford either to neglect its working-class base by ignoring bread and butter issues or to vacate too much electoral ground to the CDU and the FDP. It has to try and convince the majority of voters that it is competent at economic management and can be trusted with the defence of the national interest. Scharping's muddle over tax (see p. 54) during the run-up to the 1994 federal election awakened old fears about the SPD.

However, despite the strategic problems facing the party, the SPD continues to play a vital role in the Federal Republic. It is still par excellence a 'membership' party with just under one million members. In the Imperial Reich and the Weimar Republic, it was almost a state within a state, providing its members with a whole range of educational, cultural and sporting facilities. Willy Brandt described how, in the days of Weimar, he was enrolled in the party's sports club when very young and rapidly joined the mandolin, drama and puppet clubs as well, graduating to the SPD youth groups.[6] Post-war, the party became less all-embracing but retained a big membership. In the 1950s and early 1960s, it was still predominantly working-class but its base changed in the 1970s. At a party meeting at that time, I noted that university educated middle-class members appeared to be in a big majority. Though most union officials are SPD supporters, there is no formal link with the German unions and, with the changing social composition of its membership, there is some danger that the party will lose its connection with its industrial working-class vote.

But even at its least successful, the SPD retains the support of a third of the electorate, which means that, though it usually wins less votes at a federal level than the CDU, it is the only conceivable base for an alternative governing majority. In addition, the SPD is in government in all but two of the Länder, giving the party not only strength at regional level but also, through its control of the Bundesrat, a share of power at the federal level as well. If the risk is that, in the words of a party official, 'the SPD will become more of a Land than a federal party', its supporters and voters are able to feel that, through their party, they have an influence on local, regional and national affairs. In short, even when it is not in government nationally, the SPD nevertheless makes a major contribution to German democracy.

Like the CDU, the Free Democratic Party (FDP) was formed after the war. Its founders saw it as the successor to the old German Liberal parties. In the 1950s, when it was the coalition partner of the CDU, it was supported by farmers, the self-employed and Protestants. In the late 1960s, when it switched course in a left-wing liberal direction to form the SPD-FDP coalition, it became more of a white collar, city party. In the 1980s, when it switched back to the CDU, it turned into the party of the better educated, higher income group – those who have 'made it'. It has had a number of prominent leaders, including Theodor Heuss, the first President, Walter Scheel, Foreign Minister and later President, and Hans-Dietrich Genscher, the world's longest-serving Foreign Minister.

But it has never rivalled the CDU or the SPD. It has remained very much a third party, at times dropping perilously close to the 5 per cent electoral requirement for entering the Bundestag. As one of its MPs said in 1994, 'The FDP is in trouble – so what's new?' Even though the FDP did manage to get into the Bundestag at the federal election, it was a very narrow shave. For many years, its problem has been that of identity, its policy stance fluctuating as it has changed coalition partners. An expert on

German politics described its position as follows: 'It is close to the CDU on economic policy, though if anything keener than the CDU on pure market economy and lower taxes. It is close to the SPD on church-state relations and civil liberties and has at times been in agreement with SPD foreign policy.'[7]

However, despite its 'Vicar of Bray' behaviour, it has undoubtedly fulfilled an important function in Germany's democratic structure. It has been an almost permanent coalition partner. It has tried to act as a brake on the major governing party of the day. And, on two occasions, it has been the agent for changing coalitions. In a proportional system, there will usually be a place for a 'hinge' party, such as the FDP. But whether the present FDP, dependent as it is on CDU 'second' votes (see pp. 202–203), will continue to survive is open to question.

In 1979, a new kind of party, the Greens, burst on to the political scene. 'We are the anti-party party,' said one of its then leaders, the late Petra Kelly. Even now most of its supporters are under thirty-five, usually highly educated and still 'fed up' with the older parties. The Greens are usually described as the heirs of the protest movements of the 1960s (though some of that generation gravitated towards the SPD). As their name suggests, their main concern has been with the environment, though they were also heavily involved in the opposition to the deployment of medium-range nuclear missiles in Germany. Initially, they achieved dramatic results in Landstag elections and succeeded in getting into the Bundestag in 1983. But their underlying difficulty has been to decide what kind of party the Greens should be or, as one Green enthusiast explained to me, 'whether we are a political party at all.' This conflict, argued out with great ferocity between the so-called realists (*Realos*) and so-called fundamentalists (*Fundis*), was eventually resolved in favour of the *Realos* by the shock of the Greens' failure to clear the 5 per cent hurdle in the 1990 Federal elections. The Greens are now in coalition with the SPD in several Länder and are likely also to be a force, as the party of idealistic youth, at national level as well. At the 1994 election they won over 7 per cent of the vote thus entering the Bundestag.

The Party of Democratic Socialism (the PDS), known by both its supporters and opponents as the *Rote Socken* (or red socks), is the successor to the East German Communist party. Its lively parliamentary leader, Georg Gysi, wants it to become a modern social democratic party. It is noticeable still that it receives the support of former party members. But, at present, its main and extremely important role is to represent not just old-style Communists but all those who have lost out in the Eastern Länder following unification. With its effective grass roots organization, a legacy from the GDR, the PDS is well placed to be *the* East German regional party, and, by winning more than three individual constituencies in the 1994 Federal election, won the right to be represented in the Bundestag.

When the victorious allies occupied Germany after the war, they were surprised not to be met with a Nazi-led resistance. As Golo Mann wrote, 'With unbelieving amazement, the Allies found almost no National Socialist in a country governed for twelve years by National Socialists.'[8] It was certainly the case that, despite some continuing latent support for Hitler, at least for his pre-1940 successes, total defeat and widespread destruction eliminated the backing for Nazism. The allied authorities tried and, to some extent, succeeded in carrying out a process of 'de-Nazification', which involved hundreds of thousands and which included the removal of Nazis from public posts as well as trials (the most famous of which took place in Nuremberg in 1946) of the most prominent. But inevitably, the Allied authorities and, after 1949, the Adenauer Government found that there were not enough qualified people to run post-war West Germany and many former Nazis were brought back into public life. Well known figures rehabilitated included Alfried Krupp, who after being sentenced to twelve years' imprisonment for using slave labour, was allowed to take over his steel mills again, and Hans Globke, Adenauer's head of Chancellery, who drafted the official commentary on Hitler's anti-Jewish laws.

It is arguable that more should have been done to confront the Germans with what had happened under Hitler. Willy Brandt said: 'There was a need for reconciliation, but the evil past had to be confronted unflinchingly.'[9] Adenauer, also a resolute opponent of the Nazis, took a different view. With such an urgent need to rebuild, he believed that only ex-Nazis who had committed criminal acts and remained unrepentant should be barred from holding positions of responsibility. The then US High Commissioner, John McCloy, sympathetically likened Adenauer's attitude to that of Abraham Lincoln towards 'Southerners' after the end of the American Civil War. Both men put national reconciliation first.

The most powerful practical argument against a revival of right-wing extremism and neo-Nazism was – and remains – the stark contrast between the appalling catastrophe into which Hitler led the Germans and the prosperity and stability of the Federal Republic. However, the drafters of the Basic Law gave the German democratic system an extra safeguard. Under Article 21, parties which threaten the democratic order or endanger the Federal Republic can be deemed unconstitutional by the Constitutional Court. In addition, the Federal Office for the Protection of the Constitution (*Bundesamt für Verfassungsschutz*) provides intelligence on extremist threats to the Federal Republic. These duties have been taken extremely seriously.

On the revolutionary left, the Communists were banned in 1956, though a successor party has been permitted to exist. The *Verfassungsschutz* kept the Baader-Meinhof terrorist group and the Red Army Faction under investigation. Very controversially, it had a role in the implementation of the *Radikalenerlass* (or extremists' directive) which forced Government officials to pledge loyalty to the 'free democratic basic order'. On the extremist right, the neo-Nazi party, the *Sozialistische Reichspartei* (SRP), was banned in 1952 and, over the years, other neo-Nazi organizations have been prohibited. Sometimes, however, the authorities have formed the view that it was safer to allow non-violent groups to operate publicly, so that their activities could be more easily monitored. During the period of the Grand Coalition (1966–69), a new extremist right-wing party, the National Democratic Party (NPD), won representation in a number of Länder. But, even though it received 1.4 million votes (4.3 per cent of the poll) in the 1969 federal election, this was not enough to get into the Bundestag and its support rapidly declined.

Following unification, there has been a significant and disturbing revival of right-wing extremism. The combination of rising unemployment, social discontent and a sudden flood of asylum seekers and refugees provided an ideal breeding ground for xenophobic violence. In the latest edition of his authoritative book on the Germans, Alan Watson warns that the extremist right 'has to be taken seriously and its impact on German democracy in the few years since reunification has proved significant.'[10] The Republican Party, founded in Munich in 1983 by a former Bavarian TV journalist, Franz Schönhuber, who wrote a book extolling the virtues of the Waffen SS, of which he was a member, cleverly exploited the immigration issue and, in the Baden-Württemberg election of 1992, won 10.9 per cent of the vote. Growing support for the extremist

right took place at the same time as the dramatic increase
in racist violence (see Chapter 4), though the leaders of the
Republican Party claimed that they had no links with the
neo-Nazi thugs and skinheads involved in these attacks. No
wonder that there was great and understandable disquiet
expressed both inside and outside Germany about what
was happening. The German response, however, provided
the answer to those who questioned whether the Federal
Republic was strong enough to withstand attacks from the
extremist right. The widespread popular demonstrations
against racist violence, especially after the Mölln murders,
the tough measures taken by the Government to root out
neo-Nazi groups, and the cross-party agreement to amend
Germany's liberal asylum legislation demonstrated clearly
that, in contrast to Weimar, the overwhelming majority
was not only on the side of the Federal Republic but also
prepared to defend it. Significantly, in the 1994 European
elections, the Republican vote declined to 3.9 per cent of
the electorate and, at the federal election, to under 2 per
cent, while the numbers of racial attacks, though still much
too high, are decreasing. The continued existence of an
extremist right vote and the vicious behaviour of its violent
auxiliaries is still a matter for concern. Right-wing extremism must always be carefully watched and, where its
activities become illegal and/or unconstitutional, must be
dealt with speedily and firmly – in France and Britain as
well as in Germany. Judging from its record so far, there is
no cause for pessimism about the Federal Republic's ability
to respond effectively.

The key to the stability of the Federal Republic is the
prevailing democratic consensus. It had its roots in catastrophic defeat in the *Stunde Null* (or Zero Hour) of 1945
when the Germans had to start again from scratch. It was
nurtured by firm political leadership, by the success of the

social market economy and by the relevance, coherence and lasting strength of the democratic institutions enshrined in the Basic Law of 1949. It is expressed today at a number of levels – in politics, parliament and federal Government, in the relationship between the federal Government and the Länder (see Chapter 4), in the economic and industrial fields (see Chapter 8), and in popular support for democratic values and institutions.

The electoral system compels parties to work together. Every Government since 1949 has been a coalition of parties (though in practice the third Adenauer administration (1957–61) was so dominated by the CDU-CSU that it was a single-party Government in all but name). As one authority puts it, 'while Germans like strong and stable Governments, they do not like single-party Governments. Power should be shared, not abused. Election after election has shown this and opinion poll after opinion poll has confirmed it.'[11] Coalition government inevitably influences behaviour. The high-handed attitude of a British Government backed by an overall parliamentary majority is simply not possible within the German system. Both CDU and SPD-led coalitions have had to spend time and energy fashioning compromises with their junior partner, the FDP.

Consensus spills over not only into relations between Government and the Bundestag but also between Government and opposition. While the British House of Commons still sees its main role as a political debating chamber between a polarized Government and opposition, the Bundestag is far more a 'working' parliament in which MPs do their main work in specialized legislative committees. Even when a party is in opposition, as the SPD has been since 1982, its members often make a genuine contribution to the shape of legislation. This almost never happens in the British system.

The ability of the opposition to influence things is enhanced if, through electoral success at Land level, it is able to control the Bundesrat. The sight of the CDU Chancellor, Helmut Kohl, and the SPD opposition leader, Björn Engholm, announcing together, as they did in March 1993, a 'solidarity' package of spending cuts and tax increases to finance subsidies for the Eastern Länder may be alien to the British but is not an uncommon feature of the German political system. In 1966, the two major parties actually came together to form a big or grand coalition, and in 1994 a number of commentators believed that it was a possible outcome of that year's federal election. Although few politicians positively argued for a grand coalition, the fact that it was conceivable was a good illustration of the extent of consensus in the Federal Republic. In Björn Engholm's view, 'today, all large parties are in principle capable of forming coalitions with one another. There are in the end few differences which cannot be overcome.'[12]

There can be disadvantages in a system in which consensus is so heavily emphasized. There have been much publicized political scandals, including the mid-1980s Flick affair involving illicit payments to political parties, the 1987 Barschel dirty tricks scandal, which led not only to Barschel's suicide but the resignation in 1993 of Björn Engholm, his SPD opponent, and various resignations for tax fiddles and misuse of public funds, though those were relatively minor by the standards of most other democracies. Perhaps more important, the system can become too 'cosy' and 'in house'; valuable ideas and arguments can be stifled, genuine differences can be glossed over and contact can sometimes be lost with the voters. One of the reasons for the success of the Greens was disillusionment by some of the younger generation with the political establishment. German democracy can also be slow to adapt to change. It is arguable, for example, that some badly needed post-unification reforms such as tackling the public debt and altering the asylum laws were too long delayed. All the same, the system did, in the end, start delivering in these two areas – and did so with cross-party agreement. However, the most important strength of the Federal Republic is that, unlike the Weimar Republic, it has maintained the support of the vast majority of Germans. Despite some disillusionment with politicians, the level of voter participation remains high and opinion polls consistently show that democracy and its values continue to have overwhelming popular backing. The Federal Republic has proved to be a democracy *with* democrats.

## Chapter Seven

## THE D-MARK AND THE BUNDESBANK

'Not every German believes in God, but they all believe in the Bundesbank'

*Jacques Delors*

On the north-west outskirts of Frankfurt, there is a big, thirteen-storey block. There is nothing particularly impressive about the building. It could be one of those impersonal hotels which sprang up in most of the world's big cities in the 1960s and 1970s. Only the well guarded front gates and the name 'Deutsche Bundesbank', carved in large letters in the wall beside them reveal the importance of the institution.

For this is the home of the prestigious Bundesbank, guardian of Europe's most powerful currency, the Deutsche Mark (D-Mark). Here, every second Thursday, the sixteen members of the Central Bank Council meet on the thirteenth floor to decide German monetary policy. Their decisions are eagerly awaited not only in Germany but across Europe and in the rest of the world's financial centres. As its authoritative biographer, David Marsh, has written, 'The Bundesbank has replaced the Wehrmacht as Germany's best known and best-feared institution.'[1]

But how powerful is the Bundesbank in reality? Is its independence compatible with parliamentary democracy? How effective has it been in meeting the challenge of German unification and in responding to the pressure for European economic and monetary union? Can it continue to play as important a role in the future as it has in the past? These are questions which are asked by Germans and by other Europeans.

★

The enormous respect with which the D-Mark and its protector the Bundesbank are held is, to a considerable extent, the product of German history. The horror of hyper-inflation is deeply embedded in the national consciousness. The great inflation of 1923 and the post-war currency collapse were traumatic events which are still remembered by many living Germans. Dieter Hiss, former adviser to Helmut Schmidt and the president of the Berlin Land Central Bank, explains the importance of those two experiences: 'Germany's great awareness of the need for stability is the result of a painful learning process, still present in people's minds, which wiped out savings twice within a period of less than thirty years.'[2]

The roots of the 1923 inflation lay in the financing of the German war effort by borrowing rather than by taxation but, under Weimar, prices rocketed nearly two billion times following the resort by Governments to the printing press to pay for war reparations and for social expenditure. In 1923, the Mark became completely worthless. By 1 July, the rate of exchange with the dollar had risen to DM 160,000; by 1 August, to a million; and by 1 November, to 130,000 million. Wheelbarrows were used as wallets. A historian graphically described what happened:

> The collapse of the currency not only meant the end of trade, bankrupt businesses, food shortages in the big cities and unemployment; it had the effect, which is the unique quality of economic catastrophe, of reaching down to and touching every single member of the community in a way which no political event can. The savings of the middle classes and working classes were wiped out with a ruthlessness which no revolution could ever equal; at the same time the purchasing power of wages was reduced to nothing. Even if a man worked till he dropped it was impossible to buy enough clothes for his family – and work in any case was not to be found.[3]

The catastrophe of 1923 was partially mirrored by the collapse of the Reichsmark after the Second World War. The Reichsmark (RM), which had depreciated considerably during the war, was undermined first by the 'occupation' Mark used by the Allies and then by the American cigarette, which became an alternative medium of currency. When a semi-skilled worker's wage was only RM 80 compared to the RM 1,000 which a dollar carton of cigarettes could fetch, it was abundantly clear that, as in 1923, the majority of Germans were being forced to live at subsistence level – and that the time had come to act.

The Allied currency reform of 1948, which exchanged RM for the new Deutsche Mark at a rate of RM 10 for DM 1, officially wiped out hundreds of billions worth of savings. Yet these savings had already been undermined by the 'cigarette' economy and the new DM immediately established itself as a hard currency. One economist wrote: 'On June 21st 1948, goods reappeared in the stores, money resumed its normal function, the black and grey markets reverted to a minor role, foraging trips to the country ceased, labour productivity increased, and output took off on its great upward surge.'[4] A stable currency provided the necessary framework for Germany's remarkable recovery.

Today the D-Mark is the symbol of German economic success. It is true that it has lost two thirds of its value since 1948. But over four decades the inflation record of the Federal Republic has been better than its neighbours – and German output has increased faster. The relative stability of the D-Mark has been the guarantor not only of rising living standards and holidays abroad but of the social and economic fabric of the state. 'Other nations may live off memories of past empires, off the glory of their landscapes, off prowess in sport, in political leadership or in the manufacture of electronic chips. Germany vaunts the D-Mark, the backbone of the nation.'[5]

The power of the D-Mark was never more clearly demonstrated than in 1990. To East Germans, obtaining access to the purchasing power of the West German currency was a key objective of unification. 'If the D-Mark does not come to us, we will go to the D-Mark,' they chanted in the streets. It was this threat which was a decisive factor in persuading Kohl to support an immediate monetary union of the two Germanies at a 1 to 1 exchange rate – a decision which may·have made sense politically but which, as the Bundesbank warned, was economically highly dangerous (see below). The D-Mark thus became not only a cause and an instrument of unification but also, in East Germany, an agent of industrial change and job destruction.

When Kohl supported European economic and monetary union as part of the price for gaining French acceptance of unification, most Germans felt uneasy because they saw it as a threat to the D-Mark. In the week of the Maastricht agreement, the front cover of the weekly news magazine *Der Spiegel* carried the headline '*ANGST UM DIE D-MARK*' (fear for the D-Mark), while *Bild Zeitung*, Germany's biggest selling newspaper, proclaimed '*DAS ENDE DER MARK*' (the end of the Mark). 'The days of the D-Mark are numbered . . . This is praised in Bonn but the population thinks otherwise.' *Bild Zeitung* was right. By September 1992 only 8 per cent of West Germans and 6 per cent of East Germans believed that a future European currency would be as stable as the D-Mark. Given the past, few Germans were prepared to allow risks to be taken with their currency.

The Bundesbank's main duty, as defined by the 1957 Bundesbank Law, is to safeguard the currency, and it is from its success as guardian of the D-Mark that it derives its popularity in Germany and its reputation abroad.

The Bank has a number of instruments at its disposal in

carrying out its responsibilities. These include monitoring monetary targets, adjusting minimum bank reserves, and buying and selling government bonds and securities on the open market. However, by far the most important is the setting of interest rates, the so-called Discount and Lombard Rates, at which the Bundesbank lends money to the commercial banks. It is these rates which determine credit in Germany – and throughout Europe. By law, the Bundesbank, not the Government, decides on the level of interest rates. In this respect, the Bundesbank is independent of Government. However, its autonomy should not be overstated. The Government has the overall responsibility for economic policy. Although the Bundesbank has operational responsibility for buying and selling foreign currencies, it is the Government which has the final say on the exchange rate. And the government appoints and pays the salaries of the president and the other six members of the Central Policy Directorate. Successive Bundesbank presidents have stressed that the Bundesbank is not an alternative Government and that they are bound by law to support the economic policies of the elected Government. All the same, control over interest rate decisions gives the Bundesbank Central Council considerable economic power. Theoretically, the Government can delay changes in interest rates for two weeks: in practice this veto has never been used. This is not because Governments have always agreed with the Bundesbank's decisions. But differences are usually argued out in private. Governments do not wish to be seen to challenge publicly the authority of the Bank. Whatever the short-term inconvenience, German politicians prefer to leave tough monetary decisions to the Bank, while the voters are happy that the main instrument for preserving the value of the D-Mark has been taken out of the hands of the politicians.

The Bundesbank sees part of its job as promoting a

counter-inflationary consensus. The more it can encourage self-discipline by the main economic players, the less it has to use the interest rate weapon. But, as David Marsh rightly points out, it also occupies the role of referee: 'If it feels inflationary pressures are getting out of hand, the central bank reserves the right to confront the politicians, industrialists and trade unionists who exert the main influence on corporate Germany.'[6] On a dozen occasions, the Bundesbank and the Government have been in disagreement over interest rates or on the exchange rate – and the Bundesbank, backed by its immense prestige, has nearly always come out on top.

Some Bundesbank presidents, especially Karl Otto Pöhl, have given the impression that they alone dictate the bank's policies. The reality is different. They have to win the support of the Central Bank Council, nine of whose sixteen members are heads of regional banks. These regional representatives, some of whom, like Reimut Jochimsen of North Rhine-Westphalia, are Social Democrats, cherish their independence and cannot be relied upon to support the presidential line. Arguably, this federal power structure brings an element of democracy to an organization which is otherwise not formally accountable to any elected body.

As a member of the House of Commons Treasury Select Committee, I have had the opportunity to meet the last three presidents of the Bundesbank – Karl Otto Pöhl, Helmut Schlesinger, and Hans Tietmeyer. In contrast to most of their British and French counterparts, these three men came from relatively humble backgrounds. Rising to the top through their own efforts, each was appointed president because of outstanding competence. Despite their varying experiences and temperaments, all three have been loyal Bundesbank representatives. In their different ways, they are a remarkably impressive trio.

Karl Otto Pöhl is lucid, witty and charming. Almost permanently bronzed, he is a *bon viveur* with a young second wife. Always ready with the quotable phrase, he speaks fluent English and enjoys interviews with foreign journalists. When I and my parliamentary colleagues met him at the Bundesbank in June 1990, he dealt with our questions with authority and good humour, although he was already under considerable pressure (see below). Asked to sum up his overall judgement on unification, he replied that, on the whole, he was optimistic: 'What else could I be?'

Born in 1929 in Hanover, he had an unhappy childhood, as his father was unemployed for a long period and his mother died when he was fifteen. He left school when he was only seventeen and became a trainee journalist at a local SPD newspaper. Impressed by Schumacher, the SPD leader, Pöhl joined the party in 1948. In order to finance his university studies at Göttingen, he then worked as a freelance sports reporter, covering local football matches most Sundays. In the 1960s he was a lobbyist for the German Banking Association in Bonn before joining the Economics Ministry in 1970. His career took off under the Social Democrat Government in the 1970s when he became state secretary at the Finance Ministry and, in 1977, deputy president of the Bundesbank. Appointed president by Schmidt in 1980, he was reappointed by Kohl to serve a second term. In May 1991, he resigned, mainly because of differences with the Chancellor.

His successor, Helmut Schlesinger, then vice-president, had not expected to succeed Pöhl, as he was five years older. While Pöhl was very much a man of the world, Schlesinger was an ascetic technocrat. Somewhat ponderous in style, his strength lay in his mastery of his briefs. However, he received the Treasury Committee with every courtesy when we visited the Bundesbank in November

1992, even referring to the Queen, who had recently visited the eastern Länder, as 'Our Queen'. With his bald head and glasses, he looked very much the German professor.

A Bavarian, with connections with the CSU, Schlesinger joined the predecessor of the Bundesbank, the Bank Deutscher Länder, in 1952. When Pöhl arrived at the Bundesbank in 1977, Schlesinger had already been there for a quarter of a century. Although he shared some of Pöhl's reservations about the 1 to 1 exchange rate, he was much less controversial in public. All the same, he took his responsibilities as president of the Bundesbank extremely seriously. 'Financial and monetary stability are decisive values for our country; they must be maintained,' he said, and to prove it he raised German interest rates at a time when most European countries wanted lower ones. If Schlesinger was, by the nature of things, somewhat of an interim president, his steadiness under pressure and devotion to duty ensured that he was not an insignificant one.

Hans Tietmeyer, who succeeded Helmut Schlesinger as president in October 1993, has been described as combining 'missionary enthusiasm and formidable negotiating skills with the charm of a blunderbuss.'[7] He can certainly be brusque, but I have always found him extremely intelligent and well informed. When I saw him at the Bundesbank in June 1994, he cut short my remarks about the prospects for a more autonomous Bank of England with 'I understand that there is no consensus behind the idea of an independent Bank of England.'

Tietmeyer is a Catholic from near Münster in Westphalia, German Catholicism's most northerly outpost. He is one of a large family and in his youth wanted to be a priest. His route to the top came through the Catholic student movement and the CDU, which he joined in 1960. In 1962, he went into the Economics Ministry and, twenty years later when Kohl became Chancellor, he became state secretary at the Finance Ministry. In 1990, he was appointed by the Chancellor to the Bundesbank, becoming vice-president in August 1991. Seconded by Pöhl to help mastermind monetary union with East Germany, he was the obvious choice as president when Schlesinger retired.

Stubborn, outspoken, sometimes enigmatic, Tietmeyer is a big man in every sense. He has had a close relationship with Kohl and kept silent about the D-Mark/Ostmark conversion rate but he has not allowed his political affiliations to influence his official attitude to early European union. 'It makes no sense to speculate about the date at which monetary union could come into force,' he has warned. He is likely to fight hard for the Bundesbank's survival as Europe's most powerful institution.

Another notable figure in the Bundesbank Central Council is Professor Reimut Jochimsen, the Social Democrat regional bank president from North Rhine-Westphalia. Once a planner in Willy Brandt's office, I first met him in 1980 when he was Economics Minister in the (regional) government at Düsseldorf. An ideas man, Jochimsen enjoys nothing better than causing a stir with a controversial speech or book. In December 1991, he was the first member of the Bundesbank to express public scepticism about the Maastricht Treaty, saying in London that giving up the D-Mark without first achieving an accord on political union was 'courageous, even maybe suicidal'. It is rumoured that Kohl turned down his candidature for Bundesbank vice-presidency (appointing instead a CDU trusty, Johann Wilhelm Gaddum) because of his criticism of Maastricht. Jochimsen wrote a book in 1994 advocating a new Maastricht Treaty to put the European Union on a firmer basis.

The limits of the Bundesbank's power were clearly revealed

over unification. The Bundesbank were against immediate monetary unification: Kohl decided otherwise. The Bundesbank were against a 1 to 1 exchange rate: Kohl decided in favour. The Bundesbank supported tax increases: Kohl decided against. When faced in 1991 by evidence of rising inflation, the Bundesbank responded by raising interest rates, as it was entitled to do. But its actions, which had an impact not only in Germany but throughout Europe, were far stronger than they would have been if at least some of their advice had been taken in 1990.

Kohl's decision in favour of immediate monetary union took Pöhl by complete surprise. On 6 February 1990 he was in East Berlin for talks with the head of the East German Central Bank and was astonished to learn later that the Chancellor had already been on television to announce an immediate monetary union with East Germany. Only a few days before, Karl Otto Pöhl, echoing Helmut Kohl and the Finance Minister, Theo Waigel, had dismissed any idea of a quick union as 'fantastic'. On 5 February, even though Pöhl had discussions with both Kohl and Waigel, there had been no indication that such a move was imminent.

In fact, it is highly probable that Kohl only decided on monetary unification on the morning of 6 February, having been persuaded by East German Christian Democratic leaders the night before that it was the only way to stop massive migration to the West – and simply forgot or decided not to inform Pöhl. As one expert has put it, 'Seldom in the field of economic history had a step of such consequence been prepared with so little forethought.'[8] Indeed, so hasty was this momentous decision about the currency that it was taken without the knowledge of the Bundesbank. At a press conference three days later, Pöhl confirmed that monetary union was a decision not for the bank but for the Government. But he warned of the industrial consequences and added, 'I always advise the Government to consult the Bundesbank first.'

However, the Bundesbank's advice was overruled over the vital question of the D–Mark/East Mark conversion rate. At the end of March, the Bundesbank suggested a 2 to 1 rate, because the Council, especially Pöhl, was concerned about the impact of a more generous rate on industry and employment. But under pressure from Easterners, the Government announced a 1 to 1 rate for wages and smaller savings deposits. Pöhl made it known to the House of Commons Treasury Committee, when we saw him later in June, that the decision was bound to lead to higher unemployment, while even Tietmeyer, who was close to Kohl and helped organize the process of monetary union, agreed a year later that the Bundesbank's proposal 'would have been more favourable both for the competitiveness of East German industry and for the necessity of maintaining wage differentials.'[9]

As Pöhl had predicted, monetary union at a 1 to 1 rate led to the virtual collapse of East German industry. In order to sustain East German incomes and consumption, the Bonn Government then agreed to an unprecedented transfer of public funds, amounting to DM 150 billion, flowing from the West to the East. Kohl and Waigel, however, initially refused to increase taxes to pay for this public spending boost and resorted instead to borrowing on a massive scale. The public sector borrowing requirement rose from 1 per cent of the Federal Republic's GDP in 1989 to 5 per cent in 1994. In February 1990, Pöhl had foreseen that tax increases would be necessary and said it was shabby for politicians to talk of unification for thirty years and then, when it came, not to want to pay for it. When in May 1990 the Government set up the German Unity Fund outside normal budget procedures to transfer public monies to the East, the Bundesbank was not even informed. William Nölling, the SPD president of the Hamburg Landeszentralbank, exploded: 'The government has to stop acting as if the autonomy of the Bundesbank has been put aside for the process of reunification.'[10] Pöhl, who was in an extremely awkward position, issued a reprimand to Central Council members to stop criticizing the Government.

However, in March 1991, Pöhl himself, appearing before the economic committee of the European Parliament, made the comment that East Germany had been ill prepared for the monetary union and said that the aftermath had been a 'disaster'. These remarks were deeply resented by Kohl and led to Pöhl's resignation two months later. There is little doubt that Pöhl was right about the Government's mistakes and omissions. But the Government was working to a different agenda – preventing a mass migration from East to West and winning the federal election. It was also the case that unification and its pressures had exposed the limits of the Bundesbank's authority. When the chips were down, a really determined Government could get its way – except, of course, in interest rates.

Faced by growing fiscal deficits, a rise in the German inflation rate to over 4 per cent and by the failure of the Government to heed its warnings, the Bundesbank, led by a new president, Helmut Schlesinger, responded in the only way it could by putting up interest rates, increasing the discount rate three times in 1991 and again in July 1992. The consequence was a German recession, with falling output and rising unemployment. The Bundesbank's high interest rate policy was understandable in German terms but much tighter than was justified by conditions in the rest of Europe. The Bundesbank has been called 'The Bank that rules Europe'. In 1992–93, its tough anti-inflationary stance, adopted for German reasons, had perverse and deflationary European consequences, which led to considerable criticism of the Bundesbank by Germany's partners, especially Britain.

Since the European Monetary System (EMS) was set up in 1979, the D-Mark has been the pivotal European currency and the Bundesbank the pivotal European monetary institution. As laid down by the Maastricht Treaty, European Monetary Union (EMU) will give other European countries greater power vis-à-vis Germany by allocating the key role in monetary affairs to an independent European central bank, in which their national central bankers would be represented, and by replacing the D-Mark by a European currency. It is obvious that the Germans in general and the Bundesbank in particular have most to lose by EMU. As Hans Tietmeyer, then vice-president, said in Frankfurt in June 1991, 'United Germany has much to lose in the forthcoming re-ordering of European currencies, having one of the most successful and best monetary constitutions in the world.'[11]

The Bundesbank was taken off guard by the December 1991 Maastricht deal, as its leaders did not expect the other European countries to accept such stringent 'convergence criteria' for participation in 'Stage three' of EMU or to back an independent European Central Bank. However, in the month following the deal, the Bundesbank made public its misgivings. For example, when the House of Commons Treasury Select Committee met Helmut Schlesinger in Frankfurt in November 1992, he made it clear that the date of 1999 for monetary union was a mistake. He thought that the date 'should have been left open'. He also emphasized to us that German public opinion was hostile to EMU, as they thought it meant the 'end of the Mark'.

The waning support for EMU inside Germany, which culminated in the ruling by the German Federal Constitutional Council that the final decision on whether Germany should join monetary union would be made by the Bundestag, coincided with two major crises in the European Monetary System (EMS). First, in September 1992, sterling and the lira were forced to leave the EMS Exchange Rate Mechanism and then in, August 1993, after a wave of speculation against the French franc, the currency fluctuation bands had to be widened from 2.25 per cent for most currencies to 15 per cent.

Britain's humiliating departure from the Exchange Rate Mechanism led to an open and messy quarrel between the British Government, particularly Norman Lamont, the then Chancellor of the Exchequer, and the Bundesbank. From the moment of Britain's entry in October 1990, the Bundesbank made no secret of its view that sterling was overvalued at DM 2.95. When Helmut Schlesinger appeared to suggest in a newspaper interview in September 1992 that there was a need for a 'more comprehensive realignment' following the devaluation of the Italian lira, there was an immediate run on sterling. Norman Lamont, who had four times asked Helmut Schlesinger to reduce interest rates at an informal meeting of European finance ministers at Bath two weeks before, publicly blamed the Bundesbank for provoking the crisis. Schlesinger issued an unprecedented press statement via the German ambassador in London in which he sought to defend his position by underlining the massive support for sterling by the Bundesbank in the foreign exchange markets.

When the Treasury Select Committee questioned Schlesinger in November of that year, he and his deputy Tietmeyer were most concerned to mend Anglo-German fences. However, they insisted that, if a currency came under pressure, then the rules of the Exchange Rate Mechanism laid down that there should be a realignment. In other words, they were reaffirming the Bundesbank's view that the fundamental problem was that sterling was overvalued. If the Bundesbank was almost certainly right about sterling, the underlying cause of the French franc crisis the following year was the mismanagement of German unification and high German interest rates. Schlesinger said later the French had all the 'fundamentals on their side – except credibility'.[12] He could have added that the crisis showed that, if it comes to a conflict between its German and its European responsibilities, the Bundesbank would always put Germany first, though he would probably have tried to square the circle by saying that 'our currency is your problem'.

The Bundesbank has played a crucial role in the Federal Republic's economic success by helping to ensure that, in marked contrast to the inflationary catastrophe of 1923 and the collapse of the Reichsmark after the war, the D-Mark became the most stable currency in Europe. On occasions, as in 1992–93, concentration on bringing inflation under control has pushed up unemployment very sharply, though, in the Bundesbank's defence, it should be said that, once an economy is allowed to get out of balance, there is no painless way of restoring it.

In the German polity, the Central Bank's autonomy in monetary policy and interest rates has proved entirely compatible with a flourishing democracy. Indeed, the Bundesbank's independence in this area has strong popular support. The limits of its power and influence in the face of a determined Government were clearly shown·by what happened over unification. A number of other countries, including France, have now set up independent central banks, but the Bundesbank model, shaped by German experience and tradition, is not necessarily transferable to other democracies. The recent move towards more openness in the relationship between the British Chancellor of the Exchequer and the Bank of England is an indication, however, of the influence of Germany's example.

As to whether the Bundesbank will give up its role, as it has developed under the EMS, as the guardian of European monetary policy and of the D-Mark, the anchor currency, in favour of a European Central Bank and a European currency is problematic. Helmut Schmidt has suggested that, unless the D-Mark is replaced by a single European currency by the year 2000, the D-Mark would have become de facto the European currency. No doubt, the Bundesbank could live with that scenario. The question is whether Germany's European neighbours would agree. The rows over the British exit from the ERM in 1992 and the French crisis the following year suggest that the situation in which the Bundesbank is the unofficial European monetary authority is likely to cause continuing resentment.

## Chapter Eight

## THE SOCIAL MARKET ECONOMY: CAN IT SURVIVE?

'The success of yesterday is the defeat of tomorrow'
*Wolfgang Roth, banker and former SPD politician*

'The changing structure of production and markets require changes to, but not abandonment of, social market institutions'
*David Goodhart in* The Reshaping of the German Social Market[1]

In his comfortable office in the glass headquarters of the Federation of German Industry (BDI) overlooking the Rhine at Cologne, Ludolf von Wartenberg, the BDI's impressive general manager, took a relatively optimistic view of the prospects for Germany's social market economy. He fully accepted that structural reforms were needed: 'In a few years' time, made in Germany will be replaced by designed in Germany.' But he did not believe that the social market should be abandoned. In Frankfurt the 'whizz kids' in the German Metalworkers' Union (IG Metall) research department talked of the need to reconstruct 'the added value chain', with, for example, component manufacture going to lower cost countries, such as Poland, Hungary and the Czech Republic. They agreed with the employers that change could be achieved within the existing 'social consensus' structure.

Others are more pessimistic about the future of the German economic system. Konrad Seitz, German ambassador in Rome, has pointed out that Germany's industrial strength is concentrated in the products of the second industrial revolution, such as chemicals, cars and mechanical engineering, and is poorly placed in more modern products such as electronics, semi-conductors and computers. Critics worry about lack of innovation and dynamism, high labour costs, over-regulation, an inefficient public sector and a 'bloated' welfare state. A British diplomat told me, with just the slightest trace of *Schadenfreude*, that Germany has the 'world's oldest students, the youngest pensioners, and most expensive workers'.

But what exactly is the German social market economy? What are its strengths and weaknesses? Can it adapt to new ways of working and new global competitive pressures, especially from the Pacific Basin? These questions, especially the last one, were in my mind throughout the preparation for this book. So much flows from the answers. If Germany is economically successful, then the rest of Europe prospers. But if Germany falters, all Europeans will suffer too. It really is the case, given the predominant role of the German economy, that if Germany sneezes the rest of Europe catches cold.

The German social market system has attracted attention and support from across the British political spectrum. One commentator has put it neatly: 'The right has focused on the market, the centre on consensus, and the left on worker rights and welfare.'[2] But there has not always been a proper understanding of the distinctiveness and interdependence of the institutions which make up the social market.

A key to the social market is the concept of the company as an alliance of 'stakeholders' – employees, customers and suppliers as well as shareholders. Ellen Schneider-Lenné, an influential board member of the Deutsche Bank, which plays such an important part in German industry, explains the position very clearly.

> The objectives of German companies do not stop at maximization of the return on investment. Their philosophy is based on the

concept of the interest of the company as a whole. The company's prime objective is doubtless to secure its survival over the long term. Alongside this, however, the long-term interests of its employees, customers, suppliers, and the general public have also to be taken into consideration.

These stakeholders, including the employees, are represented on the non-executive supervisory board which approves many of the strategic decisions, especially appointments.

In contrast to Anglo-American capitalism, the German co-determination system and works council law gives labour a statutory say in the running of the shopfloor and the company. In any workplace employing more than five people, employees can elect a works council which has a right to be consulted over key issues, such as working time and redundancies. In companies with more than eight hundred employees, there is a right to information and to seats on the supervisory board.

Wherever I went in Germany, I questioned employers and trade unionists about the co-operative industrial relations, characteristic of the social market, and, with few exceptions, both groups extolled its virtues. Trade unionists stress the minimal number of days lost in strikes and the commitment of their members to their companies as well as to high living standards. One told me, 'Involved employees are essential to the progress of the enterprise.' Ludolf von Wartenberg, the BDI's general manager, said that, 'The unions are the best friends of greater efficiency and rationalization,' while managers at BMW (which in 1994 bought the British car firm Rover) confirmed to me the key role which works councils and supervisory boards play in their company. 'As partners, they help us take a long-term view,' was a typical management comment.

Capital in the German system has also been 'long-term'.

In comparison to Britain, equity markets are still underdeveloped. Only 665 companies are quoted in Germany compared with 2,200 in the UK. In the past, German firms even refused to trade their stock on the New York Stock Exchange, arguing that the requirement to publish quarterly reports was a distraction from their proper long-term concerns. Most quoted companies are dominated by a small number of large, stable investors, while company finance has come predominantly from retained earnings. In contrast to Britain, banks have been prepared to lend over the long term and, in return, have been closely involved in the company as shareholders. Studies show that UK companies have to pay out twice as much as comparable German companies to shareholders in dividends, while hostile takeovers are virtually unknown. A British industrial analyst concludes, 'At its best the German financial system allows managers to concentrate their energies on product markets without the incubus of short-term performance pressure, but with strong pressure to produce results over the long-term.'[3]

The pattern of German industry is also different from that of Britain. There are the big household names – such as Daimler-Benz, Volkswagen and BMW in motor cars, Siemens in electrical goods and BASF, Hoechst and Bayer in chemicals – which have been successful in international markets. But traditionally one of the strengths of the German economy has been in the *Mittelstand*, the small to medium businesses which 'concentrate on what they know that they do well and make sure that it is good enough to be among the best in the world.' There are 10,000 medium sized manufacturing companies in Germany compared to 1,700 such companies in Britain. Most of these firms are still family owned and have tended to think 'in decades not quarters'.[4] Both types of companies – the big and the smaller – are used to co-operating in areas which are vital to the health of the German economy. The big firms have built up relationships of trust with their suppliers, while all but the smallest firms make a contribution to the widely admired 'dual' training system (school-based and workplace courses) through compulsory membership of the regional chambers of commerce which supervise and examine company-level training.

Germany's training system is often cited by foreign companies as one of the main reasons for investing in the country, and, according to the British National Institute for Economic and Social Research, explains more than half the productivity advantage that Germany enjoys over the UK. A British trade union friend, after a visit in 1994 to study training facilities in Hamburg, wrote in highly complimentary terms of the 'deep-seated belief in German culture that makes it economic sense to train people to high standards', and concluded that the young generation in Britain needs to ask itself 'why so much less time and money is being invested in their education and training compared with that of their German counterparts'.[5] One of the answers is that, as I have found out in over twenty years visiting Germany, German employers tend to think in a less narrow and more long-term perspective than their British equivalents. British managers could learn much from the German example.

A crucial ingredient of the social market economy is the welfare state. In the view of most Germans, including employers, social welfare is not just a 'residual' or an 'add on' but an integral part of Germany's post-war success. The 1949 'Basic Law' laid down that the Federal Republic was a *Sozialstaat*. It built on Bismarckian traditions of compulsory insurance and employer responsibility for health, unemployment and pensions but added universal payments (including child benefit) and also ensured that non-employees did not fall through the net. Benefits were substantially improved under the Social Democrat-led coalitions. However, Germany has been a high per capita spender on welfare since the late 1940s and the welfare state has been strongly supported across the political spectrum. David Goodhart concludes that higher per capita spending in Germany than in Britain has 'little to do with inefficiency and more to do with national choice and the fact that spending is, in effect, hypothecated and thus independent of political-fiscal cycles.'[6]

Germany is still a high deduction, low poverty society. Germans put more into their social security system than the British but most of them take more out as well, particularly in respect of pensions (the majority qualify for about 65 per cent of their final income). Before unification, West Germany had a far smaller proportion of the population living below the official poverty line, and incomes were much less unequal than in Britain or the United States. Even today, a British visitor to the western part of Germany is immediately struck by the feeling of prosperity and well being. As an *Economist* survey of Germany in 1994 put it,

> Germany is hard to beat for the unquantifiable benefits that make a country pleasant to live in. Its cities boast pedestrianized precincts. Sleek autobahns and clean railways make it easy to get around; inter-city trains have on-board computers telling you how many minutes to go until the next stop. If you are ill, the treatment, courtesy of the social-insurance system, is among the best in the world; if you are unemployed, the benefits are among the most generous. If you are employed, the benefits are even better: high wages, long holidays and often lifetime employment. And beyond the utilitarian, German cities vie to support the best opera-houses and museums, producing a musical and artistic infrastructure unsurpassed anywhere.[7]

Early in March 1993, Graham Turner wrote an article in

the London *Daily Mail*, under the headline 'A RUDE AWAK-ENING FOR THE FAT MAN OF EUROPE', about the problems facing German industry. After visiting Daimler-Benz's Sindelfingen plant near Stuttgart, he proclaimed with ill disguised glee:

> Mercedes, like much of German industry, is weighed down with great rolls of the fat and flab which it accumulated during the decades when it was so stunningly successful . . . the scale of the overmanning is reminiscent of British Leyland in its worst days: great snowdrifts of white-collar staff, whole regiments of blue-collar workers who are now surplus to requirements and hang like millstones round the company's neck.

He also pointed to the high labour costs which were more than doubled by the social contributions made by the employer, the inflexibility of the trade unions and works councils and the inadequate spread of the Mercedes model range. He contrasted Daimler-Benz's predicament with the 'level of flexibility and commitment' which a party of German managers had found in four factories in Britain and concluded, 'If Germany is now the Fat Man of Europe – with Chancellor Kohl its perfect embodiment – Britain has become its Lean Man.' Once the nationalist crowing is stripped away, the serious subtext of the *Daily Mail* is clear: Unbridled Thatcherite capitalism had proved superior to the German 'social market' model, based, as Edzard Reuter, Chairman of Daimler-Benz (maker of Mercedes), put it, 'on a relationship of respect'.[8]

By early 1993, it was obvious that more was wrong with German industry than the impact of an economically botched unification and a Bundesbank-induced recession. 'Too fat, too heavy, too dear' is how the Hamburg weekly, *Die Zeit*, described it. Already in 1988, the BDI had launched a campaign for job flexibility and deregulation under the slogan *Standort Deutschland* (Germany as a place in which to invest), in which it pointed to the growing worldwide competition. Tyll Necker, then president of the BDI, said, 'We should repair the roof in time – during the good weather.'[9] Unhappily, during the unification boom, German companies unwisely relaxed their control of wage costs and, following the exit of Britain and Italy from the ERM and the devaluation of other European currencies in September 1992, German goods suffered a huge deterioration in competitiveness. Between 1991 and 1993, wage costs per unit of production rose 13 per cent in West Germany, more than in the whole previous eight years between 1982 and 1990 and considerably in excess of competitor nations. This had a severe impact on German traditional export industries. According to the OECD, Germany's share of world exports fell from a peak of 13.1 per cent in 1987 to 10.7 per cent in 1993.[10] 'The excellent quality of German goods and the high productivity of German workers can no longer compensate for our prices,' is how a Ruhr manager explained the situation to me. Michael Spindler, Chief Operating Officer of Apple, shocked an audience of German bankers by remarking: 'Quality is increasingly meaningless, because it can be replicated anywhere. In the future, the only difference between good and bad, winning and losing will be time-based competition.'[11] His message to Germans was that costs, after-sales services and availability were just as important as quality.

As the industrial situation grew worse, the operation, if not the principles, of the social market system began to be questioned. It was claimed that the social market was ineffective at dealing with large external shocks because, when a fast and flexible response was required, the emphasis on consensus became an obstacle. In the bargaining field, the finger was pointed at the unions for not exercising more restraint in the West during the 1990 and 1991 wage

rounds and for pressing for a speedy equalization of wages
in the East. And the cosy 'stakeholder' system of corporate
governance came under scrutiny, following some spectacular company crises and failures.

At the end of 1993, Metallgesellschaft, the metal group
and then Germany's thirteenth largest industrial concern,
got into severe difficulties, following huge losses sustained
through oil trading in the United States, and had to be
bailed out by its principal banks, the most important of
which was Deutsche Bank. The Deutsche Bank found itself
in trouble again in April 1994 when the Schneider property
group, to which it had lent DM 1 billion, went bankrupt.
The failure of Daimler-Benz's plans to diversify into aerospace also embarrassed the Deutsche Bank, which had a
dominant position on the company's supervisory board.
Critics argue that, under the German system, management
boards are given too great a freedom and that banks can
face conflicts of interest when they are both shareholders
and creditors of companies that ran into difficulties. As the
*Financial Times* commented, 'German style supervision can
shield companies from the discipline that would otherwise
be exerted by financial markets.'[12]

Questions were also being asked about Germany's welfare state. Official forecasts predicted that by the year 2000
nearly one quarter of the population will be over sixty,
compared with less than 20 per cent today, and by 2030
the over-sixties will have risen to 40 per cent, with all that
could mean for social spending. The social integration of
East Germany, which entitled inhabitants of the new
Länder to West German levels of benefit, as well as the
collapse of East German industry and the surge in unemployment, turned a potential long-term problem into a
short-term crisis of public indebtedness.

These difficulties have been exacerbated by the burden
which the social insurance method of paying for unemploy-

ment, health and pensions puts on employees and employers. In 1994, employer/employee deductions amounted to 39 per cent of gross incomes, compared to 26 per cent in 1970. Not surprisingly, employers became concerned. Writing at the end of 1993, Kurt Lauk, a board member of a Düsseldorf chemicals firm, proclaimed, 'Deep cuts in the welfare net, immediately influencing the standard of living for all citizens, are necessary.'[13]

However, while German industry's rivals were crowing over its shortcomings, the 'social market' players were restructuring and reforming the system.

The major firms took drastic action to bring their costs down. Daimler-Benz cut costs by DM 4 billion in 1993 alone and, by 1995, its workforce will have been reduced by almost 20 per cent from its 1992 level. In early 1993, Volkswagen appointed the former General Motors manager, José Ignacio López, to drive down costs by simplifying production and reducing the number of suppliers. Robert Bosch negotiated reduced wage costs and more flexible working practices. Both Mercedes and BMW announced plans to locate plants in lower-cost countries. The BMW takeover of Rover was in part a move to give the firm access to a low-cost production base in Europe. It was not just the big companies. '*Mittelstand*' firms, especially machine tool makers, rushed to simplify products, cut costs and team up with other manufacturers in marketing and customer services.

Significantly, the trade unions co-operated in these reforms. As an official at the industrial employers' economic institute described it, 'A union is like a big ship; it takes time to change direction.' But the unions, like the employers, changed direction with a vengeance. A whole series of collective agreements were reached in 1993 and 1994 which not only reduced real wages but allowed firms to deploy labour more effectively. The Munich-based IFO Institute commented in June 1994, 'During this year's pay round in West Germany the system of free collective bargaining proved its value in an extremely difficult point in time for the German economy.'[14] An IG Metall official told me, 'We have to do it. If we are to retain jobs and social welfare, then we have to be flexible.'

The result of these efforts has been highly impressive. On average, western German wages have fallen 1 per cent in real terms since the start of 1993, after rising by 4 per cent in 1991–92; and unit labour costs have fallen an unprecedented 6 per cent after rising by 7.5 per cent in 1990–92. Enno Langfeldt of the Kiel Institute argues that the centralized wages system has made for across-the-board wage restraint, while allowing more and more deals to be negotiated by wages councils. In other words, 'The system is tough enough to push wages down and flexible enough to permit special cases.'[15]

Attempts were also made by the politicians to restrain the welfare and public spending system. The first stage in health service reforms reduced costs significantly, while the 'Solidarity Pact' of March 1993 represented a genuine effort to make the West German taxpayer pay more to the East. In autumn 1993, the Rexrodt report put forward proposals to reduce costs in industry. Overall, there were enough positive signs of change for an authoritative *Financial Times* columnist to conclude that 'the institutions of the social market are proving both more supple and more resilient than many believed possible.'[16]

Even so, the combination of economic recovery and successful restructuring has not been enough to silence the critics. Herbert Henzler, chairman of the German branch of the world-wide firm McKinsey, says that the gap in production costs between German firms and firms in Asia and the

United States cannot be made up quickly. He is also concerned about the lack of innovation and dynamism: 'Not enough is coming out of our research centres. For an average young German business graduate, the idea of rolling up his sleeves, starting a business with his wife and possibly working himself to death is much too abstract even to be considered.'[17] Yet many believe that is how to create more jobs. A Düsseldorf industrialist detects a 'dramatic change in the work ethic' and argues that it is 'gradually developing into an ethic of leisure, the only meaningful prize for work.' He concludes, 'That productivity and quality of work suffer as a consequence is scarcely surprising.'[18] Reimut Jochimsen, Bundesbank board member and president of the North Rhine-Westphalia Landesbank, says that, though German industry has turned the corner, 'barely half the job has been done'.

Officials at the BDI pointed out to me that Germany employs nearly 30 per cent of the labour force in manufacturing, higher than its main rivals, and that this proportion was certain to come down. 'German industry will have to become more globalized,' says BDI general manager Ludolf von Wartenberg. More and more production is likely to take place outside Germany, especially in Eastern Europe. One in three of manufacturing companies plans to transfer part of its production outside the country over the next three years, according to a survey conducted by the German Chamber of Trade and Industry. Siegfried Utzig, senior economist at the BDI, explained why: 'German companies have to reduce total costs by 20 to 30 per cent to remain competitive in global markets. Eastern Europe, which is on their doorstep, offers them a chance to do this.'[19]

Despite considerable restructuring amongst the *Mittelstand*, Germany's former 'hidden champions', there continue to be worries about their long-term health. Gunter

Kayser, director of the Bonn-based Institute for Mittelstand
Research, claims that these small and medium-sized firms
are losing their capacity to innovate, and that some of their
traditional strengths, such as producing high-quality products for market niches, may become handicaps.[20] Their
Japanese rivals may simply beat them on price and availability. The international management expert Charles Handy
highlights the fragility of their family base: 'Many of the
*Mittelstand* businesses are now approaching that third generation . . . They are losing their innovation thrust, the family
is becoming lazy, or greedy, or both. Some are looking for
ways to sell.'[21]

Some argue that one of the problems for the *Mittelstand*
firms is the lack of a developed equity market. If Germany
had such a market, new managers could be hired and
capital raised more easily. Pressures for change are, however, slowly building up. Younger people are inheriting
about DM 200 billion per year, a proportion of which
many would like to invest in equities. Until now, pensions
in the private (and public) sector have been unfunded, which
means that companies can use the cash. If pensions become
funded, the money would be available to boost the stock
market, it is estimated, to three times its present size.
Arguably industry, particularly small and medium-sized
firms, would benefit.

Concern about Germany's lack of innovation is shared
by the BDI. 'The innovation process is too slow,' I was
told. The Government line is that the problem is not so
much in basic research but in its application. However, a
recent analysis of worldwide patented inventions showed
that Germany's share slipped back from 18.4 per cent in
1987 to 16.2 per cent in 1990.[22] A number of commentators
I met suggested that many of the post-1968 generation are
'anti-technology'. A leading industrialist, whose wife votes
Green, told me that he believed that there was a growing

bias against the introduction of new technology in Germany.

Germany's higher education system is also frequently criticized. The jibe about the country having 'the oldest students in the world' is in part justified, as the average length of study is seven years and many German graduates do not enter their careers until their late twenties. An anxious father, himself a university professor, complained that his son, who had no academic ambitions, would be twenty-eight before he left university. When I asked what kind of job his son wanted to get, I was told that he would look for 'safe' employment in a bank. When I suggested that he might start his own business, his father shrugged and said, 'Young Germans like my son expect to get a responsible job in a large organization.'

The large increase in numbers of students (well over 1.5 million) has been concentrated in the arts subjects or mechanical engineering. David Goodhart, former *Financial Times* correspondent in Bonn, argues that 'young people in Germany have not taken as readily to the new electronics-based disciplines as their counterparts in the US and Japan, and there is now an old-fashioned feel to much of the technology of everyday life in Germany from telephones to newspaper production.'[23]

There is even concern that technical change may be eroding the advantages of the much vaunted 'dual' training system. Significantly, in March 1994 there were 250,000 apprenticeship vacancies in the western Länder (while in the eastern Länder applicants out-numbered available apprenticeships by two to one). The explanation of the Federal Labour Ministry is that the vacant places are in 'old-fashioned' industries, no longer so much in demand, and that many more young men and women now prefer to seek training in the commercial or trading sector.

It is clear that a major threat to the social market system is the high level of unemployment – 2.5 million in West Germany and a further 1.2 million in the East. The restructuring of West German industry has been partly achieved by shedding one million jobs, while in the East the disastrous impact of the collapse of the East German industrial base has been masked by an expensive system of training and employment creation schemes. Dr Werner Tegtmeier, Under Secretary of State at the Federal Ministry for Labour and Social Affairs, says that 'the high unemployment rate will remain the central challenge for economic and social policy'. Unemployment benefit is a heavy cost to employers and employees and to the taxpayer. At the same time, a large pool of potential workers remain idle, which is economically wasteful and socially divisive. Dr Tegtmeier estimates that in 1994 over six million extra jobs were needed to achieve full employment.

The debate on where these extra jobs are likely to come centres on two areas – the service sector and part-time employment. For such an advanced country, the service sector is still relatively underdeveloped. The visitor to Germany is quickly struck by the restrictive opening hours. Shops, even corner ones, must close by 6.30 p.m. on weekdays and 2 p.m. on Saturdays. In the UK, anyone may advertise as a builder, plumber, or vehicle mechanic. In Germany, however, a person may not offer services to the public unless he or she is registered with the appropriate craft chamber. Restrictive regulations like these have now been extended to the Eastern Länder where there are widespread complaints against 'red tape'. 'They want us to become capitalists almost overnight – but then force us to adopt a whole lot of new bureaucratic rules,' was one comment. Pressure from East Germany could help modify excessive regulation. Social change – the trend towards single-parent families, the growth in female employment (still well below the British figure), the ageing population – also creates demand for new services.

Germany has far fewer part-time jobs than many of its competitor countries. At 15 per cent of overall employment, the proportion is lower than in the United States and Japan and well below that of the Netherlands and Scandinavian countries. Roland Berger, a leading business consultant, has argued that, if the labour market was more flexible, every fourth job could be part-time, as in Britain. The main obstacles, according to Dr Tegtmeier, are 'the prejudices which exist at the lower and middle management on the side of the employers as well as on the side of the employees.'

The question is whether the social market system will prove flexible enough to enable Germany to re-equip and modernize, while, at the same time, bringing together East with West Germany. The industrial restructuring and shake-out of 1993 in the west is impressive evidence that, under pressure, the system can adapt to change. However, there is a big reform agenda ahead, including the need to improve innovation, the need to restructure the big firms and strengthen and loosen up the *Mittelstand*, the need to reform higher education and rebalance training, and the need to create more jobs in service industries and part-time employment by deregulation and greater flexibility. But the underlying strengths in the social market economy, above all that capital and labour can 'pull together' in a 'stakeholder' company, provide a strong 'consensual' framework within which to combine wealth creation with social cohesion. I remain optimistic about the ability of German social market institutions to respond to global competition.

## Chapter Nine

## GERMAN INTELLECTUALS AND DEMOCRACY

'To loosen rigid political conditions, disseminate impatience with reality, strew about, blow away the fog of ideologies of justification, all necessities on the road to the constitution of liberty, which intellectuals have to accept'

*Ralf Dahrendorf in* Society and Democracy in Germany

'Brandt had Grass, Schmidt had Popper, Kohl has Kohl'
Der Spiegel, *3 July 1994*

To coincide with the festival to celebrate the German Romantic movement held at the South Bank in London during the autumn of 1994, a debate was held on the question 'Is Romanticism dangerous?' A distinguished Anglo-German panel discussed whether it was safe to celebrate the movement's 'pursuit of paradise', or whether it was a dangerous force which could run out of control. Their almost unanimous consensus was that it was a historical to blame the Romantic movement for Hitler and that today's Germany was a strongly pluralist democracy which could readily encompass a number of differing ideas, including romantic ones. Professor Michael Stürmer, Chancellor Kohl's historical adviser, argued that the Romantic movement was, in any case, merely 'a German variation on a European theme' and that, because Germany was 'a collection of tribes', there was no such thing as a German national psyche, rather a plethora of German attitudes and views. All the same, though Germany's *'Dichter und Denker'* (poets and thinkers – and musicians and painters too) have been widely and justly admired for their artistic and cultural achievements, their contribution to the creation of a thriving German democracy in the late nineteenth and twentieth centuries has received a bad press. In his magisterial *Society and Democracy in Germany*, first published in 1965, Ralf Dahrendorf discusses the role of German 'intellectuals' – those who create, distribute and apply culture. He distinguishes three attitudes: the 'classical' attitude which explicitly accepts the ruling power and social conditions of the times; the 'romantic' attitude which withdraws from the 'dirty face of action'; and the 'tragic' attitude of the 'outer' emigrants 'who cannot sleep when they think of their country, until in the end they have to leave it in order to survive'. His concluding judgement is a harsh one:

> If intellectuals as a group and in their diversity fail to provide the sting and doubt that accompany every form of distribution of power, every single political decision, but rather embrace the powerful or sever all ties to them, then their effect is not democratic. German intellectuals have had this effect.

How justified are these criticisms? What is the contribution of German intellectuals today? How far do they assist in the development of a healthy and pluralistic German democracy?

The European Enlightenment tended, especially in its French version, to be anti-establishment and critical of the status quo. By contrast, the German *Aufklärüng* was more respectful of authority. Many of its participants were civil servants or professors whose salaries were paid by Government. Leibniz was a public servant at the Courts of Brunswick and Hanover, Kant a professor at Königsberg in East Prussia, Goethe a prominent official at the Saxe-Weimar Court and Lessing ended up as a librarian to the Duke of Brunswick. But German intellectuals were not only influenced by self interest and position. They also believed, with some justification, that social improvements could be achieved with the assistance of enlightened rulers. In his essay on 'What is Enlightenment', Kant argued that, though it was not as yet an enlightened age, Germans were living 'in an age of enlightenment', in which it was possible, given benign rulers, to achieve progress.

Kant had a good point. His own King, Frederick the Great of Prussia, was the personification of the *Aufklärung*. Although a superb general and strategist, whose spectacular victories and cunning diplomacy helped establish Prussia as a major European power, he was delighted to be known as the 'Philosopher of Sans Souci'. At Sans Souci, his charming rococo summer residence at Potsdam, he surrounded himself with writers, artists, musicians and philosophers, including the French savant Voltaire, with whom he had an intense relationship, and himself wrote poetry, history, philosophy and played the flute. Frederick also saw himself as a King who governed according to the principles of the Enlightenment. Acting not as an arbitrary despot but as 'the first servant of the state', he introduced religious toleration, rationalized the administration, reformed the legal system, improved education and developed the Prussian economy. His reputation as a ruler was so great that, in the second half of the eighteenth century, Prussia was thought to be the model European state.

Immanuel Kant, who is usually regarded as one of the greatest philosophers of modern times, was not politically involved at all. His life was unremarkable, being almost entirely devoted to scholarship; his routine was so strict that it was said that the housewives of Königsberg could set their watches by the time of his passing during the course of his daily walk. But this reclusive academic transformed philosophy. In his *Critique of Pure Reason* he sought to put forward a theory of knowledge which would provide a synthesis between the rationalism of Leibniz and the empiricism of Hume. In his introduction, he wrote, 'There can be no doubt that all our knowledge begins with experience. But though all our knowledge begins with experience it does not follow that it all arrives out of experience.' When we make judgements about the world, human understanding is dependent, according to Kant, on certain *a priori* concepts: 'Thoughts without content are empty, intuitions without concepts are blind.' Turning to ethics, in his *Critique of Practical Reason* he sought to establish 'the categorical imperative' as a basis for morality. Kant argued that the principles which govern moral action are categorical – that is to say that we ought to follow these without qualification, as though they are universal laws. He also said, in a revolutionary formulation, that human beings should always be treated as ends and never as means. In his *Critique of Judgement* he added to these works a theory of aesthetics, in which he gave a special role to the imagination. It is the use of imagination which defines the aesthetic judgement.

If Kant's existence was austere, Goethe was deeply involved in the world. It has been said that his greatest masterpiece was his own life: he was poet, dramatist, novelist, occasional scientist, painter, enthusiastic traveller and lover as well as courtier and minister. His romantic novel *The Sorrows of Young Werther*, published when he was twenty-four, was an international sensation. It was quickly translated into all the major European languages, young men dressed *à la* Werther, in blue tail coats and yellow waistcoats, and there were even Werther-style suicides. When Goethe met Napoleon at Erfurt in 1808, Napoleon claimed to have read Werther seven times, though he criticized Goethe for allowing a confusion of motives in Werther's suicide. However, Goethe's greatest achievements were his lyric poems, his novel *William Meister*, and his two-part verse drama *Faust*. Together with

Friedrich Schiller, the brilliant playwright and poet, Goethe put German on the European map as a literary language.

Most of the stars of the *Aufklärung* were consciously cosmopolitan, believing that the principles of the Enlightenment provided a passport which transcended national boundaries. Lessing, the dramatist, claimed that he was not interested in patriotism because 'it would teach me to forget that I must be a citizen of the world', while Schiller said that 'I write as a citizen of the world who serves no prince. At an early age, I lost my fatherland to trade it for the whole world.'[1] Goethe saw science and literature as a substitute for national pride:

> A comparison between the German people and other peoples awakens in us painful feelings, which I try to overcome in every possible way, and in science and art I have found the wings that enable one to rise above them, for science and art belong to the world and before them the barriers of nationality disappear.[2]

But one of Goethe's contemporaries, his mentor and critic, Johann Gottfried von Herder, who, at the instigation of Goethe, came to Weimar as Ecclesiastical Superintendent, took a different tack. In his *Another Philosophy of History* and *Reflections on the Philosophy of the History of Mankind*, Herder rejected the universalism of the Enlightenment in favour of cultural pluralism. He took the view that people could only realize themselves fully if they belonged to an identifiable group or culture with roots in tradition, language, culture and common historical memories. Although he was a pluralist, he also stressed the importance of cultural autonomy. Germans must be Germans, and not third-rate Frenchmen. 'Germans, speak German! Spew out the Seine's ugly slime,' he exhorted.

It was partly to the ideas pioneered by Herder that nineteenth-century German intellectuals turned. In the Germany transformed first by Napoleon and the ideas of the

French Revolution and, after 1815, by the Industrial Revolution and the rise of Prussia to predominance, intellectuals felt the need of a more romantic, nationalist vision which would validate the identity and worth of Germans. It was not necessarily a political position – most of the Romantics agreed with Hölderlin: 'What do I care about the shipwreck of the world, I know of nothing but my blessed island.'[3] But the emphasis on the charismatic individual who realizes his potential, even at the expense of society's laws and conventions, was a move away from the Enlightenment.

A key figure in German nineteenth-century thought was Georg Wilhelm Friedrich Hegel, so much so that Golo Mann argues that what 'Napoleon was to the political history of the period Hegel was to its intellectual history.' Hegel's ambitious and sometimes obscure attempt to explain the whole of human existence in terms of historical change and development – the process of 'world spirit realizing itself' – has been vigorously denounced as an apologia for Prussian authoritarianism and as a forerunner of twentieth-century totalitarianism. The German philosopher Arthur Schopenhauer remarked that 'governments make of philosophy a means of serving their state interests, and scholars make of it a trade', while Karl Popper, in his brilliant wartime polemic *The Open Society and its Enemies*, wrote that Hegel's only aim was to fight against the open society and thus 'to serve his employer, Frederick William of Prussia.'[4] It is certainly true that the state plays a crucial role in the Hegelian system: 'The state is the Divine idea as it exists on earth.' But to Hegel 'state' did not mean just the government but referred to the community as a whole. His argument was that human beings could only be free when they lived in a society organized on rational lines – one which had freedom of expression, the rule of law and trial by jury and which was ruled by a constitutional monarch. But those who came after him, including both Marxists and Nazis, used Hegel's ideas for their own purposes.

It would be wrong to put all the blame on German intellectuals for the failure of the 1848 revolution and of the Prussian parliament in the 1860s to establish a liberal democracy in Germany. But, as the distinguished American historian Gordon A. Craig argued, the stress on the development of the exceptional individual, on the role of the state, and on the German nation as a unique cultural expression meant that Germany entered the twentieth century without the kind of democratic tradition that might have enabled it to withstand the problems that were ahead, above all the 1914–18 war, the economic dislocations of the 1920s and 1930s and the rise of Hitler.[5]

Post-war German writers and artists were faced not only by the destruction of the war but also by the distortion and manipulation of German culture by the Nazis. Words like '*Volk*' and '*Heimat*', so important in the past, were no longer usable. Folk songs, dances and local customs were 'out'. Patriotism was a dirty word. A further problem was that many intellectuals had been killed or had emigrated, while some of those who remained had made concessions to the Nazi regime.

The 'literature of the ruins', which tried to come to terms with what had happened, was given direction when two left-wing writers, Hans Werner Richter and Alfred Andersch, founded the '*Gruppe 47*'. This 'mobile academy' brought together writers, poets, critics and playwrights from all over Germany, including Heinrich Böll, Günter Grass, Hans Magnus Enzensberger, and Uwe Johnson. Learning from what they perceived as the 'ivory tower' attitudes of German intellectuals in the Weimar period, they decided that writers should play a part in shaping the new German democracy.

The two outstanding figures were Heinrich Böll and Günter Grass. Böll, who was a Rhinelander, wrote a number of novels, including *The Clown* and *Group Portrait with Lady*, in which he was critical of post-war German society and of the aspiring and conforming middle class. He was sympathetic towards the student rebels of 1968 and was fiercely attacked in the right-wing press, especially *Bild Zeitung*, for publicly calling for a fair trial for the Baader-Meinhof gang. In *The Lost Honour of Katherina Blum*, Böll described how a young woman was destroyed by a tabloid newspaper because she was suspected of sheltering a terrorist. Very much a moral leader of liberal and radical Germany, in 1972 he became the first German since Thomas Mann to win the Nobel Prize for literature.

Günter Grass's dominant theme was the failure of Germans to come to terms with their Nazi past. Grass comes from Danzig (now Gdansk in Poland) and the beautiful Baltic city – 'the venerable city of many towers, city of belfries and bells' – forms the background to three of his novels, *The Tin Drum, Cat and Mouse* and *The Dog Years*. *The Tin Drum* is the story of Oskar, a dwarf with a drum, growing up in a city controlled by the Nazis. His drum is a powerful instrument, breaking shop windows and reducing Nazi rallies to open air dances. In the 1960s, Grass, like many other intellectuals, became committed to the SPD under the charismatic Willy Brandt, whom he described as a man 'who gives his melancholy deadlines'. In *From The Diary of a Snail*, which is partly a campaign journal, he made the case for reform policies: 'What's progress? Being a little quicker than the snail.'

In an interview with John Ardagh, the German critic and poet Hans Magnus Enzenberger describes the optimism of the 1960s:

Intellectuals in the 1960s felt strongly about the injustices and rigidities in German society, and we fought hard against them – with some success. We made an impact in those days. Thanks in part to the student revolt of the 1968 period, certain barriers have been broken and Germany has become a more open, tolerant and informal society, more so than ever before in its history, and an easier place to live in.[6]

The late 1960s and the 1970s saw a renaissance of German cinema. A number of outstanding talents, such as Alexander Kluge, Volker Schlöndorff, Margarethe von Trotta, and Rainer Werner Fassbinder, produced films which dealt with social issues, and explored German themes. Kluge's *Yesterday's Girl* is about a young Jewess from the GDR who fails to establish herself in the materialist West. Schöndorff filmed both *The Lost Honour of Katherina Blum* and *The Tin Drum*, while his former wife, Margarethe von Trotta, made a notable film, *The German Sisters*, about the relationship of a female terrorist with her sister. Fassbinder, who died from a cocktail of cocaine and sleeping pills in 1982, made a series of moving films about outsiders – the doomed love of a Moroccan *Gastarbeiter* and an elderly Munich woman in *Fear Eats the Soul*; the destruction of a woman accused of having an affair in his adaptation of Fontane's nineteenth-century novel *Effi Briest*; the hopelessness of homosexual love in *Fox*; and the rise to success at great personal cost of a woman in post-war German society in *The Marriage of Maria Braun*.

Werner Herzog's films are not directly about German society: as in *Fitzcarraldo*, he deals with larger-than-life characters, pursuing impossible dreams in the German romantic tradition. But Edgar Reitz has produced two social dramas for television – *Heimat* and *The Second Heimat* – which have been seen all over the world. The first traces the history of Germany in the twentieth century through the story of families in a farming village in the Hunsrück.

It shows how these villagers accepted but were little touched by the Nazis, arguably a realistic view of what happened. In *The Second Heimat*, Reitz looks at a group of young artists and intellectuals in the Munich of the 1960s and 1970s. He plots changing attitudes, from coming to terms with the older generation's catastrophic errors about Nazis, to sex, drugs and rock and roll, the events of 1968 and the Baader-Meinhof gang. The *Heimats* are more than social documentaries; they are great creative works of fiction.

In contrast to the elections of the 1960s and 1970s, at the 1994 election the 'intellectuals' were not much in evidence. True, the East German novelist and satirist Stefan Heym stood in Berlin and won a constituency for the PDS, wearing a beret and entertaining crowds with readings from his works. But, as an article in *Der Spiegel* pointed out,[7] only the veterans among the left-inclined intellectuals were at all involved in the campaign. Younger writers and philosophers kept out, while some favoured the right.

Even the old campaigners of the 1960s felt uncertain and uninspired. Walter Jens, the highly respected literary critic from Tübingen and a member of the *Gruppe 47*, asked of the SPD: 'Why don't they have any utopian dreams any longer?' Günter Grass, who had campaigned so tirelessly for Willy Brandt and even helped draft his speeches, came to Berlin to help drum up support for the social democrat Wolfgang Thierse, who was opposing Stefan Heym. But although he praised Thierse, he was highly critical of the SPD which, he told the meeting, he had left because of its asylum policies. So critical was he that someone from the audience understandably asked him, 'Why, then, are you at this SPD election meeting?' In 1990 Grass was strongly against unification because he did not trust the Germans, given their past, to cope with it.

The SPD Chancellor candidate, Rudolf Scharping,

made considerable efforts to cultivate the intellectuals. At a big rally in Dortmund he urged them 'not to stand on the sidelines' and he set up smaller 'ideas' meetings to meet writers and creative artists. Although many of them believed it was 'time for change' and were personally sympathetic to Scharping, the *Zeitgeist* was against the kind of commitment the generation of the 1960s had shown to Willy Brandt. As *Der Spiegel* put it, the intellectuals 'have lost their utopian dreams and visions and their store of ideas has been depleted ... The intellectuals complain about the provincial politicians, while they counter by pointing out how far removed from reality are the dwellers in ivory towers.'

How much does this fading commitment really matter? For guidance, I turned to Ralf Dahrendorf, whose judgement on German intellectuals is quoted above and who is one of the best known political thinkers in Europe. His distinguished Anglo-German career includes being a Professor of Sociology at the University of Konstanz in the 1960s, a federal minister in the Brandt coalition Government, an EC Commissioner, Director of the London School of Economics, and now Warden of St Antony's College, Oxford. Dahrendorf gave a more pessimistic verdict than I had expected. He looked back to the Brandt period as a time when there had been 'a climate of critical integration' which had been good for democracy. Today he is concerned that too many intellectuals in Germany hold positions which are publicly financed. Even those who work for the media are dependent either on public money or on powerful chains like the Springer Group. 'The problem is that nobody wants to endanger their position,' he said. He also argued that there are some 'alienated' writers who feel that their views are ignored because they do not belong to the present establishment.

The 'alienated' certainly includes a number of intellectuals in the east who, like Heiner Müller, Stefan Heym and Christa Wolf, remained in the GDR and hoped to create a more democratic East Germany. The Christa Wolf affair was a public reminder of the difficulties that East German writers faced in the united Germany. In the summer of 1990 Christa Wolf published a short novel, *What Remains*, which was a thinly disguised autobiographical account of how a writer who had protested against the deportation of the East German singer, Wolf Biermann, was shadowed by the Stasi. She was fiercely attacked in the weekly *Stern* as a 'national cry-baby', while Frank Schirrmacher, now cultural editor of *Frankfurter Allgemeine Zeitung*, condemned her for not having published the book earlier and denounced her 'authoritarian' personality.

I put the Dahrendorf thesis to Peter Glotz, one of the SPD's leading theoreticians, in his Bundestag office the day after the 1994 election. He was concerned that some intellectuals were turning to the right and that there were even signs of a revival of romantic nationalism. 'It may not be just a normal swing back to the right but something more worrying,' he told me. Yet the main thinkers of the right, conservative historians like Michael Stürmer and Hans-Peter Schwarz, who are attempting to define German national interests in the post-unification era, can scarely be described as dangerous. And even if they were, there is not much evidence that Chancellor Kohl, who has never been over-impressed by intellectuals, takes their views very seriously. When I asked Thomas Kielinger, an influential independent-minded conservative journalist, about the attitudes of the intelligentsia, he argued that the media were 'predominantly left wing'. These conflicting assessments about the direction of intellectual thought suggest that a new, more pluralistic balance may be emerging.

Writing from Berlin during the 1994 election, a correspondent from the London *Times* commented on the mood of mutual misunderstanding between the politicians and the 'thinkers'. 'The realization that this is normal in a stable democracy, and that the priestly role of poets and thinkers was partly an expression of insecurity, has not yet penetrated the nation's booklined studies.'[8]

Arguably writers in the 1990s, such as Patrick Süskind, are concentrating on the themes of private life – love, marriage, death – and leaving political and social themes to critics and commentators. As the *Economist* puts it,

> it is not surprising that so many of the newer German novelists are happier these days to sit out political literary controversies, and are content to be writers, not prophets . . . They avoid big themes and sermons in favour of imaginative experience, art and learning and private life . . . Novelists keep themselves out of the pulpit and the issue of German unification out of their books, not least because that issue is often on German front pages.[9]

But there is still a vigorous debate going on about the implications of unification in the historical, foreign affairs and even the economic communities – although it has been perhaps a little slow in getting going. This debate is being conducted, however, not by literary figures but by experts in the field. It may be true, as Ralf Dahrendorf argues, that many intellectuals work for publicly financed organizations – as researchers, academics, and teachers. But the German system allows for diversity. Regional Government is usually in different political hands from central Government. Conflicting opinions are voiced in the media. Each party has its own research institute. Employers and unions finance 'think tanks'. So the '*Dichter und Denker*' of the 1990s, be they writers, critics, commentators, or experts, are involved, if in a less dramatic way than in the 1960s, in safeguarding German democracy.

Part Three

# IMAGES OF GERMANY

## Chapter Ten

## GERMANY'S ROLE IN THE WORLD:
## GOOD PARTNER OR 'SPECIAL PATH'?

'In the future Germany will find itself compelled on objective grounds to make its foreign policy, and also its European policy, more self-centred, more tightly budgeted and less flexible than it has been, all in the service of a rather narrowly defined national interest'[1]

*Hans-Peter Schwarz, Professor of Political Science and Contemporary History, University of Bonn*

'It [Germany] will choose not to choose. True to its foreign policy tradition, the Federal Republic will try to do a little of everything. Sowohl-als-auch ("as well as") or, in the immortal words of Yogi Berra, "If you see a fork in the road, take it"'[2]

*Timothy Garton Ash,
Fellow of St Antony's College, Oxford*

United Germany is larger, potentially more powerful and freer to act than the old Federal Republic. It also has a more central geographical position in Europe, with nine neighbours and a capital only an hour away from the Polish border. With one eye on the past, Germany's neighbours ask how it will use its new status. Is united Germany back in the old '*Mittellage*' role, manoeuvring erratically between East and West? A writer in *The Independent* put the point bluntly:

The problem of Europe is still above all the problem of Germany's relations with her neighbours ... It is the titanic task, which neither the Germans nor their neighbours have yet succeeded in carrying out, of creating structures to accommodate the energies and legitimate ambitions of that people and to balance their fears and dreams between East and West.[3]

There is another view which emphasizes not German strength but German weakness. The united Germany has many more external demands being made of it, at a time when it is wrestling with the problems arising from German unification and the need to make its economy more competitive. So far from being ready to take on new responsibilities, many Germans are uneasy about their country becoming a nation-state again. A poll of German opinion in 1991 showed that a majority of respondents favoured Switzerland or Sweden as a role model. Writing in the summer of 1993, two Germans argued:

> The notion of the new Germany embarking on a sinister power drive seems absurd, while that of a relaxed, united country able to juggle the many demands on its new political system seems unrealistic. Germany is powerful, but regrettably not powerful enough to fulfil all that is expected of it.[4]

How powerful is Germany? What are its foreign policy objectives? Is it a power with national interests or a post-national democracy, committed to European union? Will it still be tied to the West or will it seek accommodation with the East? Is it really a threat to its neighbours or rather, as Germany's friends believe, a force for peace and stability? These are legitimate questions to which Germany's neighbours are entitled to have answers.

In terms of its population, size and economy, Germany is now the most powerful nation in Europe. Yet Germany is no superpower. As Kurt-Georg Kiesinger, then Federal Chancellor, observed back in 1967, a united Germany would have a 'critical size . . . too big to play no part in the balance of forces and too small to keep the forces around it in balance by itself.'[5]

The nearest Germany gets to superpower status, at least within Europe, is through her economic power. For many European countries, Germany is the biggest market, the magnet which attracts their goods. The Bundesbank's monetary policies create a virtual D-Mark zone in Western Europe and have a major impact on European countries, as Britain, France and Italy found to their cost in 1992–93.

However, there are obvious limits to German economic power. As Helmut Schmidt has often pointed out, German GNP is a long way behind the United States and Japan. United Germany's share of world output in 1993 was about 7.5 per cent, compared with 27 per cent for the United States and 16 per cent for Japan. As the world's second biggest exporter, it is also very dependent on what happens in overseas markets. In the 1990s, Germany is burdened with the DM 150 billion a year cost of unification and with the restructuring of the West German economy. This internal preoccupation has implications for external policy, especially as regards loans, grants and subsidies to other countries. Cheque book diplomacy, practised so freely in 1990 to secure unification, will be used more sparingly in the future.

In the autumn of 1994, I heard General Klaus Naumann, the Chief of Staff of the Bundeswehr, explain to an Oxford audience that German security interests could only be achieved in alliance with its partners. The successor to Scharnhorst, Gneisenau and Moltke was very much the embodiment of the Federal Republic's 'citizen' army, modest, politically as well as strategically aware, and tactfully wearing a red poppy in the buttonhole of his suit. Though German troops are still, as Naumann told us, 'well equipped, well trained and well motivated', the Bundeswehr has been reduced from 600,000 to 370,000. German military power is still tightly circumscribed, by the Federal Republic's reaffirmation of its commitment not to acquire atomic, biological or chemical weapons and also by the limitation placed on the use of German forces, except for defence purposes, by the Federal Basic Law.

The long and fierce debate in Germany about whether Bundeswehr units were able to participate in UN military assignments outside Western Europe is an indication of how seriously Germans take the lessons of their history. Many SPD and Green Party activists are passionately opposed to German 'out of area' deployment, which they see as the thin end of the militaristic wedge. 'Never again' is both their hope and their plea. Attempts by the SPD leadership to shift the party position in favour of deploying German troops on UN missions abroad met with fierce opposition, and support was given to only a very restricted, 'humanitarian' participation in UN blue beret operations. However, faced by a series of decisions on German involvement, Chancellor Kohl, who took the view that the constitution allowed 'out of area' deployment under UN auspices, cautiously committed German military personnel to the UN operation in Somalia, to UN embargo-monitoring activities in the Adriatic, and to AWACS air reconnaissance over Bosnia. His argument was that Germany could not shirk its UN obligations, especially as it was seeking a seat on the Security Council. The government's actions were taken to the Federal Constitutional Court at Karlsruhe by the SPD parliamentary group and, in the case of the AWACS involvement, by the FDP group as well. In a historic ruling, on 12 July 1994, the Constitutional Court said that German forces could participate in both peacekeeping and peacemaking exercises of the UN, either acting directly under the Security Council or as part of NATO or WEU operations in order to implement UN decisions. In welcoming the judgement, Kohl emphasized the cautious German approach: 'We will decide on a case-by-case basis. We are not going to create a mood of "Germans to the front".'

Like the old Federal Republic, the new united Germany does not believe in 'going it alone'. The most distinctive feature of modern German foreign policy has been its 'multilateralism'. German leaders, like Chancellor Kohl and Foreign Minister Kinkel, pride themselves on being 'good partners' – partners in the European Union, in NATO, and in the UN. They have set their face firmly against the idea of so-called '*Renationalisierung*' (or the 'renationalizing' of German foreign policy), partly because they strongly believe in co-operative policies and partly because 'multilateralism' has served the Federal Republic so well over the past forty years. Membership of NATO has guaranteed German security, while membership of the European Union has underwritten German prosperity. They see no reason why the new, post-Cold-War problems cannot also be dealt with within a multilateral framework. 'German foreign policy does not need to be reinvented,' said Wolfgang Ischinger, head of the planning staff at the German foreign ministry.[6]

Yet there are fresh problems, especially in the East. The collapse of the Soviet Union and the old Soviet Empire has created a zone of instability on Germany's new eastern borders. The prospects for a stable Russian democracy are uncertain. If Germany is still geographically part of the West and is firmly linked to the West through a whole host of institutions, its more central position following unification, combined with the power vacuum in the former Soviet Empire, has created more responsibilities for the united Germany. At the same time, the European involvement of a United States that is under domestic pressure and looking to the Pacific Basin is becoming increasingly problematic. Some German foreign policy specialists argue that, in the circumstances, German national interests need to be more clearly defined. They believe that the old Federal habit of 'muddling through', associated with the former Foreign Minister Hans-Dietrich Genscher, will no longer be adequate, especially as German resources have not increased to match Germany's new responsibilities.

However, to talk in those terms still remains profoundly shocking to some Germans. When during a lecture tour in Germany in early 1994 I argued the case for more pro-active German leadership, I met with considerable opposition. Many Germans, particularly of the younger generation, saw the Federal Republic as a post-national European state, committed to a united Europe. Words like 'leadership' and 'national interest' smacked too much of Germany's unhappy past. The idea of the Federal Republic as an exemplary democratic country has also appealed to Poles, Hungarians and Czechs, as it has also to many in the West, especially to social democrats and liberals attracted to the German commitment to social consensus. In the 1970s and 1980s, the Federal Republic seemed a model European state, perhaps *the* model European state. In the 1990s, united Germany, wrestling with the problems of unification and finding it difficult to absorb large numbers of foreign immigrants and refugees, sometimes appears a more ordinary country. As Timothy Garton Ash remarked, 'At times, it seems as though the Federal Republic has grown in size but shrunk in spirit.'[7] Even so, the genuine idealism about a peaceful, co-operative, democratic Germany remains.

In late November, following the narrow victory of his party in the 1994 federal election, Karl Lamers, foreign policy spokesman for the CDU/CSU parliamentary group, came to London to speak at meetings, organized by the Federal Trust and by the Royal Institute of International Affairs, on the controversial policy paper on the future of European Union which he had prepared for his party group. Lamers, who was thin and ascetic-looking, spoke with great intensity on a subject about which he obviously cared passionately. But the importance of the meetings lay not so much in Karl Lamers's eloquence or the strength of his commitment to European integration but in the fact that his paper was signed by Wolfgang Schäuble, 'floor leader' of the CDU/CSU group, and had received the tacit support of Chancellor Kohl himself.

Joachim Bitterlich, a senior foreign policy adviser to Kohl, commented: 'You must bear in mind two signals about this document. First, it is an appeal to all Europeans to continue European integration. Second, it is a warning that Germany, situated in the heart of Europe, cannot accept zero progress at the 1996 review conference.'[8] The message of the Lamers paper was that Germany was still committed to further European integration. Those in Britain who had hoped that popular hostility to giving up the Deutschmark in Germany and pressure from countries like Poland, Hungary and the Czech Republic to extend the European Union eastwards would weaken Chancellor Kohl's determination to push ahead with European integration were to be disappointed.

The controversial proposal in the document was the concept of a 'hard core' of five countries – Germany, France, Belgium, Luxembourg and the Netherlands – which would press ahead with closer integration, even if other members were unable or unwilling to follow suit. Not surprisingly, the idea that a few countries would go ahead not only with monetary and economic union but with political union as well aroused alarm amongst those countries not selected for the 'hard core', especially Spain, Italy and Britain.

Lamers explained the rationale behind a 'core group': 'If a smaller group of countries presses ahead with particularly intensive and far-reaching economic and political integration, this group or core has a centripetal or magnetic effect on the other countries.' This had been the way that European unification had proceeded in the past and Lamers believed that, if the core countries, which broadly corresponded to those able to meet the Maastricht convergence criteria, agreed to set up a European Central Bank and establish a single currency, then it would have an effect on the rest who would be encouraged to join later. In a rebuke to the British, Lamers pointed out that those who, like John Major, favour 'variable geometry, can hardly object to the formation of a "hard core".' He also quoted Chancellor Kohl's remark: 'The slowest ship must not be allowed to determine the speed of the convoy.'

In his paper, Lamers stressed the importance of the traditional Franco-German relationship – 'the core of the hard core'. For Germany, commitment to European integration is partly a reassurance to France that a unified Germany will remain linked to its partners in the West, particularly France. The Germans are very much aware of French fears that an enlarged Community, especially one taking in the Scandinavian countries and the countries of Central and Eastern Europe, would become a looser grouping of states in which the united Germany would predominate. That is one reason why Helmut Kohl, quoting Konrad Adenauer, says: 'The unity of Germany and European unification are two sides of the same coin.' That is why he was so insistent on the agreement on European Union signed at Maastricht and why he wants to go ahead with closer political integration following his narrow election victory. He believes that 'German unity as a historical event will be wasted if we don't press ahead in parallel with the European unity.' Kohl's European commitment is broadly shared by most of the political establishment, including the SPD leadership. But there is some opposition, especially in Bavaria. The Prime Minister of Bavaria, Edmund Stoiber, who won an emphatic Landtag election victory in September 1994, has said 'Europe is more than the European Community. I want a single confederation. That means that the nation states maintain their dominant role, at least as far as internal matters are concerned.'[9]

There is also growing popular scepticism about some aspects of European integration, especially the single currency. According to the Allensbach poll carried out in June 1994, 73 per cent of Germans believe that membership of the European Union is a good thing but 74 per cent are against a European State and 70 per cent are against a single currency. As Arnulf Baring has put it, 'The Deutschmark is not only a currency, it is a symbol of German self confidence. Germans – unlike the British or the French – are short of national symbols.'[10]

In July 1994, Volker Rühe, the German Defence Minister from the CDU, told the Poles that Poland would join NATO by the end of the decade. He also said that he saw no prospect of Russia and Ukraine ever being able to join. This was not the first time that Volke Rühe had set the 'cat among the pigeons'. Outspoken, highly ambitious and extremely intelligent, Rühe believes that Germany's first priority should be the East. Giving the Alistair Buchan Memorial lecture in March 1993, he said: 'The reconstruction of the East must take precedence in policies of the European Community.' Rühe's view was that it was wrong to 'advance the inner perfection of the EC without also opening up the East.' And he floated the idea that prospective members might join NATO first. 'Economic hurdles that present members of the EC can hardly jump across must not become insurmountable obstacles to membership in NATO.'

Volke Rühe's foreign and security policy initiatives infuriated Klaus Kinkel, the FDP German Foreign Minister,

and irritated Chancellor Kohl who suspected Rühe of
being after his job. But Rühe was making a valid point.
Having stable democracies on its eastern borders is a vital
German interest, so Germany should be a strong supporter
of bringing the 'reform democracies' of Poland, Hungary,
the Czech Republic and Slovakia into the European Union
and NATO. The question, implied by Rühe, is whether
there is a conflict between widening in the East and
deepening in the West.

Germany's past in the East is an unhappy one. To the
Slavs, the German 'Drang nach Osten' was highly aggressive.
As the Oxford historian A.J.P. Taylor luridly put it, 'For a
thousand years from Charlemagne to Hitler, the Germans
have been "converting" the Slavs from Paganism, from
Orthodox Christianity, from Bolshevism, or merely from
being Slavs; their method has always been the same –
extermination.'[11] For generations of Poles, the Germans
were understandably always seen as a threat. With co-
operation from Russia and Austria, the partitions of Poland
in the eighteenth century removed Poland from the map.
During the Second World War, Hitler's occupation of
Poland was exceptionally barbarous. Proportionately, the
Poles had the highest losses of any occupied country and
the Holocaust took place primarily on Polish soil.

Willy Brandt's Ostpolitik was the opposite of this old
German drive to the East. It was a policy of reconciliation,
détente and peace with the Federal Republic's eastern
neighbours. If the key to the policy lay in Moscow, its
crowning moment was Brandt kneeling in Warsaw before
the memorial to the ghetto uprising, the dramatic symbol
of the new Germany. Timothy Garton Ash, in his brilliant
revisionist history In Europe's Name, is sympathetic to
Václav Havel's criticism of Ostpolitik: 'It signified, of
course, the first glimmer of hope for a Europe without
Cold War and iron curtain; yet at the same time – alas – it

more than once signified the renunciation of freedom, hence of a basic condition for any real peace.'[12] Garton Ash argues that, because the Federal Republic's priority was to negotiate with governments, it sometimes strengthened inadvertently the hand of their regimes at the expense of their peoples. All the same, it is difficult to imagine the great events of 1989–90 without *Ostpolitik*.

After German unification and the collapse of the Soviet Empire, the unified Germany, still linked to the West but bordering on Poland and the Czech Republic, has new responsibilities in the East. Ironically, given the past, it is primarily to the Federal Republic that Poles, Czechs and Hungarians look for help in transforming their countries and 'joining the West'. Already, a third of Eastern Europe's total trade with the industrialized West is with Germany; and the Germans are the obvious champions of the entry of these countries into the European Union and NATO. As far as Germany is concerned, over 50 per cent of its exports go to Western Europe: exports to Eastern Europe and Russia combined are still under 6 per cent. Although the economic importance of these countries to Germany is bound to increase, their prime importance is political. Stability on its eastern borders is obviously a key German interest. Many Germans fear the prospect of mass migration from the East, if people are forced westwards as a consequence of economic collapse. More positively, strengthening democracy in their countries and bringing them into the 'clubs' of the western industrial democracies, such as the European Union and NATO, ought to be top priority for Germany – and Europe – over the next few years.

There is an old European fear of a German agreement with Russia at the expense of others. In his chapter on the Germans in his book *The Europeans*, the Italian journalist Luigi Barzini reported a conversation with André François-Poncet, the French High Commissioner, who said,

'Suppose the Germans came to an agreement with the Russians. They did it after the First World War at Rapallo. They did it in 1939 (the Hitler-Stalin pact). We all know that every time they came to an agreement with the Russians they arrived in Paris.' Yet Germany is too attached to the West and Russia is too unreliable a partner for the development of a special relationship with Russia which excludes the rest of Europe. The Kohl-Gorbachev accord of 1990 established the basis for cordial relations and subsequently Germany has given considerable assistance to Russia. But helping Russia is too big a task even for Germany and will require a joint effort by the European Union, the United States and Japan.

For the present, Germany has to choose between Russia and the 'reform democracies'. Jochen Thies, foreign affairs editor of the conservative paper *Die Welt*, argues that from 'a historical, moral and political perspective Poland, the Czech Republic and Hungary matter for Germany more than Russia' because they represent a *'cordon sanitaire'*.[13] The three countries, according to Thies, are a buffer against surprise attack from Russia, against incidents of the Chernobyl type and against migration from the former states of the USSR. Karl Kaiser, foreign affairs expert, said that 'Germany has pushed European borders further east' by negotiating immigration control treaties with Poland, Hungary, the Czech Republic, Slovakia, and Romania, while visa requirements have been abolished for Poles, Hungarians, Czechs and Slovaks. In Brandenburg, Saxony and Bavaria, I was told about how German firms are relocating their production in Hungary, the Czech Republic and Poland, where costs are cheaper, and also about the concept of 'Euro-regions', crossing the borders between the Czech Republic and Poland. German relations with these two countries and with Hungary and Slovakia are good.

At the same time, German political leaders have been

acutely aware of the historical sensitivities. The Polish writer Andrzej Szazypiorski commented that, whereas previously the Poles had been afraid of the Germans coming with guns, now they were afraid of them coming with cheque books.[14] Between September 1990 and October 1993, the Germans provided nearly 50 per cent of total aid to countries in Central and Eastern Europe and they are continuously urging their European partners for a larger contribution. 'You and the French must help these countries too – it is in your interest as well as ours' is a habitual German cry.

The nearer these countries get to becoming members of the European Union, the more difficult the situation is likely to be. Their cheaper imports could threaten German jobs, while freeing the German labour market to Poles, Czechs and Hungarians could create problems inside Germany. Opening up the European Union to the East will put an intolerable strain on the EU budget and the CAP. The German taxpayer, who had footed the bill for unification, will not want to fork out again. As a German diplomat remarked, 'stability doesn't come cheap'.

The argument between opening up the EC to the East and further European integration is not yet resolved. Most German politicians hope that they will be able to do a bit of both. Even if to foreign policy experts that may seem too much '*Sowohl-als-auch Politik*' (or having it all ways) that it is not very different from the foreign policies of other western democracies, like the United States, Britain and France. Germany's European partners can rejoice that events since 1990 have, if anything, reinforced German links with the West. German politicians are trying to open up the EU and NATO eastwards rather than make special deals of their own. The laudable Federal Republic tradition of being a 'good partner' is still very much alive – and the bad old German tradition of 'Sonderweg' (or special path) seems dead and buried. The united Germany is in no way a threat to its neighbours and should be encouraged by its partners to play a more prominent role as a force for peace and stability in Europe and the UN, including becoming a permanent member of the Security Council.

Chapter Eleven

## BRITAIN AND GERMANY: THE OPPORTUNITY FOR PARTNERSHIP

'Britain is now an underdeveloped country'
*Helmut Schmidt in conversation with the late Peter Jenkins*

'Since the unification of Germany under Bismarck . . .
Germany has veered unpredictably between aggression
and self-doubt'
*Lady Thatcher in* The Downing Street Years

In March 1991, John Major, in his first speech as Prime Minister outside the United Kingdom, addressed a distinguished German audience at the Konrad Adenauer Stiftung, the Christian Democrat think-tank in Bonn. His speech was carefully crafted. He congratulated Chancellor Kohl, with whom Mrs Thatcher had had such glacial relations, on the 'enormous skill and quiet authority' with which he had 'steered' German unification. In contrast to Mrs Thatcher, he committed Britain firmly to a constructive role in the European Community: 'My aims for Britain in the Community can be simply stated. I want us to be where we belong, at the very heart of Europe, working with our partners in building the future.' And, referring as Mrs Thatcher would never have done to the links between the Conservative Party and the Christian Democrats, he said, 'As like-minded parties, we can achieve great things together in Europe and for Europe.' His address was clearly a bid for a new beginning between Britain and Germany.

Despite this promising start, in subsequent years Anglo-German relations improved very little, if at all. From a

German point of view, the British, under Mr Major's
leadership, have proved almost as awkward and unreliable
as they were under Mrs Thatcher, as demonstrated by the
two 'opt outs' at Maastricht in 1991 (one out of the single
European currency, the other the Social Chapter) and
the rows over qualified majority voting and the European
Commission Presidency during 1994. The outrageous treatment of Germany and the Germans by the xenophobic
British tabloids remains a source of irritation to the Germans, who are still extremely sensitive to outside opinion.
For its part, the British Government publicly and noisily
blamed the Germans for Britain's humiliating exit from
the Exchange Rate Mechanism (ERM) in September 1992.
A British specialist on Germany, writing in April 1994,
concluded that 'relations between Britain and the Federal
Republic . . . were by 1993 among the worst between any
two western states, considered close friends.'[1]

Yet, running alongside these irritations and tensions, there
are also substantial common interests. This chapter attempts
to put Anglo-German relations into perspective by examin-
ing the historical background and post-war developments.
It also analyses not only the weaknesses but also the
strengths of the relationship, and puts forward suggestions
as to how it can be improved.

British relations with Germany are still clouded by history,
above all by two world wars. British and German graves
in Flanders, Northern France, Normandy, Italy, and North
Africa bear witness to the human cost of those conflicts.
Inevitably, this immediate past colours the attitude of some
Britons, particularly of the older generation.

But it is often forgotten that the Anglo-German antagonism, which was so harmful to the peace of Europe in the
first half of the twentieth century, was of relatively recent
origin. In the eighteenth and nineteenth centuries, dynastic,

political, economic and cultural links between Britain and
the northern states of Germany were close. From 1714
onwards the British monarchs were Hanoverians, who
spoke German, married Germans and were closely involved
in German politics.

In the middle of the eighteenth century, Frederick the
Great of Prussia, whose mother was a sister of George II,
became Britain's main continental ally. During the Seven
Years War (1756–63), while British generals won decisive
victories over the French in Canada and India, Frederick's
military genius, bolstered by a large British subsidy and an
Anglo-Hanoverian army in north-western Germany, kept
the armies of France, Russia and Austria at bay in the
centre of Europe. In his testament to his nephew, his
advice was not to start another war but instead to try and
persuade Britain to pay Prussia to keep out of one. In the
Napoleonic wars, Prussia was more often than not allied to
Britain. At the battle of Waterloo, it was the opportune
arrival in late afternoon of the Prussian army, under Mar-
shal Blücher, which, as Wellington himself acknowledged,
sealed Napoleon's fate.

In the first half of the nineteenth century, a third of
Britain's European exports went to the German states.[2]
The Germans bought sugar, spice, coffee and tea from our
colonies, and, as Germany industrialized, coal from our
mines, and steam engines, textile machinery, rails and other
manufactured goods from our factories.

Liberal Germans admired the industrial might and parliamentary institutions of Britain. Particularly in northern
cities like Hamburg, the middle classes imitated English
fashions.[3] The conservative upper classes were also enthusiastic about '*der englische Lebensstil*'. To live like an 'English
gentleman' was all the rage. When Crown Prince Frederick
of Prussia married Princess Victoria of England in 1856,
Berlin went wild.

British historians were influenced by the scholarship of Ranke and Mommsen. British poets, novelists and philosophers were impressed by the German intellectual flowering.[4] Samuel Coleridge, who visited Germany in 1797, led the way. He was fascinated by Goethe, studied Kant, and translated Schiller. Thomas Carlyle, the chief Germanist of his age, wrote biographies of Schiller and Frederick the Great, translated Goethe and was strongly influenced throughout his life by German literature and philosophy. Later, in the middle of the nineteenth century, George Eliot and her husband, G.H. Lewes, introduced German thinking, including the ideas of Hegel, to the British academic world.

German unification, however, led to a cooling in Anglo-German relations. The British professed to be in favour of the principle but German nationalists were dismayed by the failure of Britain to give practical support to the cause. The British had been on the side of Denmark in 1864 and backed Austria in 1866. Although neutral in the Franco-German war, they had supplied French ships with ammunition to blockade German ports. In his *History of Germany in the Nineteenth Century*, Heinrich von Treitschke denounced 'the most sacred principle of the British, the principle that England alone is entitled to deceive other powers.'[5]

For their part, the British were shocked by the methods used by Otto von Bismarck to achieve unification. At a conference in 1864 on the Schleswig-Holstein question, the British Foreign Secretary, Lord Clarendon, is said to have left the room overcome with an almost physical nausea at Bismarck's lack of scruple. Bismarck himself admired Britain for having fought for and won imperial supremacy. But, given British isolationism, he did not believe that she would be a reliable ally. Had not Frederick the Great been shamefully deserted by George III and his leading Minister, Lord Bute, at the end of the Seven Years War? In any case,

Victorian Britain could usually be ignored on the continent of Europe. In 1865, he quipped: 'The thunders of Albion are no longer backed by lightning charges; even children do not fear them.' However, though Bismarck's sometimes unscrupulous diplomacy may have upset the British, he had no wish to fight Britain or indeed any other country once unification had been achieved.

It was the rapid growth of German economic and military power under his successors which so alarmed the British and led to the 1914–18 war. Whereas Britain produced over twice as much steel as Germany in 1860, by 1914 it produced less than half. British leaders perceived the new German might, particularly the expansion of their fleet, as a direct threat to her position as a world-wide imperial power. In a famous memorandum to his Foreign Secretary, the British diplomat, Eyre Crowe (who was married to a German), warned that 'Germany is hostile to Britain and distinctly aims at playing on the world's political stage a much larger and much more dominant part than she finds allotted to herself under the present distribution of material power.'[6]

Imperial Germany, under Kaiser William II, found the British position hypocritical. Had not the British carved out an empire for themselves? Why should they try and stop the Germans doing the same? It was Winston Churchill himself who admitted: 'We have got all we want in territory, and our claim to be left unmolested enjoyment of vast and splendid possessions, mainly acquired by violence, largely maintained by force, often seems less reasonable to others than to us.'[7] To German eyes, Britain's attitude to Germany was irrational. In 1914, Bethmann Hollweg, the German Chancellor, in an emotional farewell to the British ambassador, blamed the British for the outbreak of the war: 'It was in London's hand to curb French revanchism and Pan-Slav chauvinism. It has not done so, but has, rather, egged them on. And now England has actively helped them.'[8]

Modern warfare and modern propaganda encourage hate between nations. In Britain, virulent anti-Germanism was at its height during and immediately after the First World War, while the Germans, resenting the allied naval blockade, saw Britain as the main enemy. Yet, at the front, soldiers on both sides were inclined to respect each other's fighting qualities. According to George Orwell, the reaction of the British troops was that 'they brought back a hatred of all Europeans, except the Germans whose courage they admired.'[9]

In what the German historian Golo Mann has called 'the darkest chapter' of German history from 1933–45, the Germans allowed themselves to be led by an evil adventurer into another world war, once again with Britain as a prominent opponent.[10] Hitler may have thought he could do a deal with Britain whereby Germany agreed not to challenge Britain's imperial role in return for a free hand on the Continent. But few appeasers (there were many, including J.M. Keynes, the famous economist, who had thought that the settlement imposed on Germany by the Treaty of Versailles was far too harsh and was storing up trouble for the future) could agree to abandon the whole of central and eastern Europe, let alone France, to their fate. Given Hitler's aims and actions, renewed Anglo-German conflict was inevitable.

In the bitterness of war, British public opinion made little distinction between the Nazis and the Germans. Intellectual justification for this view was given by the historian Rohan Butler in his book *The Roots of National Socialism* which tried to establish connections between Nazi theorizing and German philosophy. How far did the German people come to hate the British? Christabel Bielenberg, an

Englishwoman married to a German lawyer, who spent the war in Germany, wrote in her autobiography, 'Goebbels never succeeded in making the Germans hate ... I had never heard a cheer go up when an allied bomber came crashing down in flames.' Her conclusion was, however, that, after over a decade of Nazi rule, the Germans 'had become an ignorant demoralized insensate mass and I could only be grateful to the few who had shone out reassuringly like beacons.'[11] She was referring to the unsuccessful German resistance to Hitler – soldiers like Claus von Stauffenberg and Henning von Tresckow; Social Democrat leaders like Julius Leber and Carl Mierendorf; aristocrats like Helmuth von Moltke and Adam von Trott – all of whom paid for the failure of the July 1944 uprising with their lives.

After the war, the British made an important contribution to the building of German democracy. As early as 1946, in his famous Zürich speech, Winston Churchill said that there can be no revival of Europe without 'a spiritually great Germany'. The British helped establish the German electoral system (a compromise between the proportional representation of the Weimar Republic and the British 'first past the post' arrangements); they backed German federalism; they insisted on a non-political civil service; and they advised that the German trade unions should be set up on an industrial basis. German friends sometimes remark that it would have been better for the British if they had applied some of their ideas to their own institutions.

In the 1950s, despite left-wing opposition to German rearmament, British Governments helped prepare the way for German participation in a western alliance. Anthony Eden's initiative, which led to the setting up of the Western European Union, was decisive. In the 1960s, Britain's belated campaign to join the European Community was supported by Germany and British entry in 1973 owed much to the strong backing of the then Federal Chancellor, Willy Brandt. Today, Germany is not only Britain's NATO ally and fellow member of the EU but also its chief trading partner.

Yet, although Britain and Germany, two of Europe's most important states, are partners in Europe's two most important institutions, their relationship has been marred by a series of tiffs and spats. The underlying cause of these quarrels is Britain's reluctant Europeanism and uncertainty about its role in the world. Additional reasons are British concern about united Germany's potential power and resentment about what is perceived as an exclusive and predominant Franco-German relationship. For their part, the Germans see the British as an unreliable and carping partner. When, on the night of the 1994 German election, a news flash came through from Helsinki that the Finns had voted in a referendum to join the European Union, the German TV reporter said that they did not intend 'to play the part of the arrogant outsider like the British'.[12]

The 1960s were a watershed in post-war Anglo-German relations. Before 1960, Germany had to some extent been learning from Britain. After 1960, it was Germany which forged ahead, particularly economically. Germany may have backed the British application for membership of the Common Market. But it was the support of a more important for a less important partner. German political leaders – Schmidt and Brandt as well as Adenauer – also made it quite clear that the French relationship came first. And, during the 1970s, Germans began expressing their disappointment with Britain as a member of the EC.

The Anglo-German Königswinter Conference, the brainchild of a formidable Anglophile, the late Frau Lilo Milchsack, is a gathering of British and German politicians, journalists, diplomats, academics, bankers, industrialists and trade unionists which has been meeting annually for over forty years. As such it provides a unique vantage point from which to view the attitude of the German liberal establishment towards Britain. The overwhelming impression is one of regret that the British have proved to be such reluctant Europeans. In 1978, I listened to Richard von Weizsäcker, later to be Federal President, warning that Britain's German friends were 'worried, disappointed and shocked' by our negative and self-centred conduct as a member of the Community.

The criticisms of Theo Sommer, distinguished editor of *Die Zeit*, are typical:

> Successive Labour and Conservative governments have exposed us to constant bickering about Britain's financial contribution. We have seen an oil giddy Britain blocking a Common European energy policy; a Britain emulating de Gaulle's empty chair tactics when it came to determining the value of the 'Green Pound'; a Britain foiling the Community's efforts towards establishing a common energy policy; a Britain being difficult about electing the European Parliament; a Britain cold shouldering the European Monetary System; a Conservative Prime Minister raising the wild spectre of 'identikit Europeans' to block progress towards 'a more perfect union' ... a Britain which, in the words of *The Sunday Times*, behaved all too often like a man who joins a club, imbibes cheerfully at the bar every evening but is curiously absent each time when it is his turn to stand a round of drinks.

Then there was the Thatcher factor. Mrs Thatcher was not only hostile to European integration; she was also viscerally anti-German. She admired their post-war recovery, the might of their industry and their capacity for discipline and hard work. But, as someone whose formative years were spent during the war, she never threw off her distrust of the Germans. Unification aroused all her old fears.

It is evident from her memoirs that Mrs Thatcher was strongly against unification and tried, though without success, to build up an alliance with President Mitterrand to delay it. At the December 1989 Strasbourg European Council, Mrs Thatcher describes a meeting with François Mitterrand. After Mitterrand had observed that the Germans were a people 'in constant movement and flux', Mrs Thatcher produced from her handbag 'a map showing the various configurations of Germany in the past, which were not altogether reassuring about the future.'[13]

The 'Chequers Memorandum', leaked in the *Independent on Sunday* in July 1990, revealed that Mrs Thatcher had a confidential meeting in March 1990 with historians and German specialists at Chequers about the implications of unification. Although the majority were optimistic, considerable concern (almost certainly by Mrs Thatcher) was expressed about underlying German characteristics. Some highly unflattering attributes were alleged to be 'an abiding part of the German character', including 'angst, aggressiveness, assertiveness, bullying, egotism, inferiority complex, sentimentality'. It was said, probably by Mrs Thatcher, that a tendency to overestimate their own strengths and a capacity to kick over the traces were reasons for misgivings about Germany's future. It was suggested, again probably by Mrs Thatcher, that the way in which the Germans currently used their elbows and threw their weight about in the European Community showed that a lot had still not changed.[14]

In her memoirs, Mrs Thatcher makes it clear that she agreed with Nicholas Ridley, then Secretary of State for Industry and a leading supporter of Mrs Thatcher, when he complained in a notorious *Spectator* interview in July 1990 about the dangers of Germany becoming 'so uppity'.[15] He described economic and monetary union as 'a German racket designed to take over the whole of Europe' and, when asked whether Chancellor Kohl was not preferable to Adolf Hitler, replied: 'I am not sure I wouldn't rather have the shelters and the chance to fight back than simply being taken over by economics.'[16] Mrs Thatcher tried to retain her faithful ally, who was merely saying aloud what she believed, but, after considerable pressure, Ridley was forced to resign.

I shall never forget Mrs Thatcher's behaviour at the Königswinter Conference's fortieth anniversary dinner which she gave for Chancellor Kohl in March 1990, the year of unification. In her speech she gave no hint that she understood the historical significance of German unity. It was noticeable that Mrs Thatcher and Chancellor Kohl hardly addressed a single word to each other during dinner. Mrs Thatcher was, however, overheard telling the former German ambassador that it would take another forty years before the British would forgive the Germans, a sentiment which obviously did not go down well with her guests. Remarks like that – not to mention Nicholas Ridley's interview and the Chequers Memorandum – caused great offence and continue to be remembered in Germany. As Thomas Kielinger put it in *The Independent*, 'Germany has been a valuable partner in all forms of collective leadership for forty years – and still there comes Mr Ridley as if he just stepped out of 1945.'

In his Bonn speech in March 1991 John Major tried to make a new beginning. His personal relationship with Chancellor Kohl has been consistently good. But his efforts to improve Anglo-German relations were undermined by the growing influence of the so-called 'Euro-sceptics' in the Conservative Party, as demonstrated by the two Maastricht 'opt outs', and by the impact of unification on European monetary policy. When Britain was forced to leave the European Exchange Rate Mechanism (ERM) in September 1992, the Prime Minister and the Chancellor turned on the German Government, even though they

knew perfectly well that the Bundesbank was responsible
for interest rate policy. They sought to shift the blame
from their mistaken policy of going into the ERM at too
high an exchange rate on to the Germans. As Edward
Pearce wrote in the *Guardian*,

> With the blaming of Germany there is no end. If Britain
> misapplies and screws up the ERM, it is a German betrayal. For
> about 24 hours senior British ministers seemed wholeheartedly to
> adopt the tabloid style. They sought to shift blame for their own
> high interest rate high pound error upon an ERM that was
> unable to protect it from gravity and upon the nation most
> involved in that institution.[17]

The British blackballing in June 1994 of the Belgian
Prime Minister, Jean-Luc Dehaene, the candidate of the
Germans and the French for President of the European
Commission in succession to Jacques Delors, was in part a
demonstration by John Major to his 'Euro-sceptics' that
Britain still had clout in the European Union. But it was
also a protest against what the British saw as yet another
Franco-German 'fix'. It had repercussions. The quarrel in
the summer of 1994 over BSE or 'mad cow disease' should
have been nothing more than a typical 'tabloid' spat.
Following fears about the impact of BSE on humans, the
Germans banned the import of British beef. Despite the
fact that the market for British beef in Germany was small,
there was a big inter-governmental row. British MPs
complained that the move was in retaliation for John
Major's use of the veto against Jean-Luc Dehaene and the
then British Agriculture Minister, Gillian Shephard, wrote
to the European Commission complaining that the move
was illegal. Although Bonn dismissed the link between the
ban on beef and the EC Presidency, the *Financial Times*
reported on the first of July that the German Foreign
Minister, Klaus Kinkel, in London for talks, was calling for
a 'European solution' to the beef issue and that the two

countries were making progress in the search for a new EC president. The question both sides ought to have been asking themselves is how such a fierce storm could have blown up over such a relatively minor problem, when relations between the two countries were meant to be so good.

Bosnia was obviously a much more important issue and here clashes of viewpoint between the two countries arose more out of differences in responsibility and a shared feeling of frustration in Europe's glaring failure to bring peace to the region. Germany's insistence on the recognition of Croatia and Slovenia in December 1991 irritated the British. As the *Economist* commented,

> with a holier than thou arrogance that grated, Germany has frogmarched its reluctant EC partners into recognition of Croatia and Slovenia . . . Germany has been passionate about recognizing Croatia and Slovenia but is not ready, allegedly for constitutional reasons, to take part in an international force there to keep the peace.[18]

In 1993, the British Government, with 2,500 troops on the ground, did not take kindly to criticisms in the German press that Britain was aiding the aggressors in the conflict. The British ambassador wrote a forceful defence in the conservative paper *Die Welt*. For their part, the Germans, who took in 300,000 refugees from the war zone, resented British claims that Britain was doing more than Germany to help the people of Bosnia.

Britain and Germany are both trying to come to terms with their changing positions in Europe and the world – and this uncertainty is reflected in their relationship with each other. United Germany has become more pivotal and has more responsibilities, while, in the post Cold War world, Britain has lost its key role as the USA's partner in the Atlantic alliance and has still to find its feet in the European Union. The British nostalgia for the war, which

Germans find so distasteful, is as much about Britain as it is about Germany. A perceptive article in *The Independent* pointed out,

> Victory over Hitler's Germany was Britain's last act as a true world power. As such it remains the British establishment's most precious asset in promoting a sense of what it means to be British. Remaking the past allows for a more favourable impression of what the nation stands for than the tawdry reality of contemporary Britain.[19]

The British are still uncertain about the role which they want a bigger, geographically more central and potentially more powerful Germany to play. As a Wilton Park Paper noted,

> Whether Germany's partners really want Germany to assume a greater political role in world affairs as they ostensibly claim is, however, debatable. They are as much wedded to the old *status quo* as Germany is and still think in terms of a politically docile and generous Germany when they call the political shots and Germany underwrites them financially.[20]

Yet if many of the British are apprehensive about German strength, they are also critical about German weakness.

The Germans are also unsure about their new role and, faced by instability in Eastern Europe and the former Soviet Union, need understanding friends to help them. It is true that the American and the French relationships have been much more vital to them in the past than the British one. The Garland cartoon in the *Spectator* in August 1992 says it all: John Major has a huge photo of Helmut Kohl on his desk, while Kohl has a tiny photo of John Major on his. Yet, at a time when the focus of American interests is beginning to turn away from Europe, Germany cannot afford to neglect its friendship with Britain. Even if it is only a medium sized power, it is still Europe's third most important country after Germany and France. And, despite all the tiffs and spats, there is a large area of shared experience and common interest between the two countries.

At the final session of the Königswinter conference at Cambridge in April 1994, an unusual discussion, initiated by British participants, took place on the subject of Anglo-German relations. It was clear from British speeches that this debate had been triggered off by the xenophobic response of the tabloid press to the Prime Minister's invitation to Germany to join in the 1995 celebration for the fiftieth anniversary of the end of the war. One *Guardian* journalist, clearly shocked by the shrillness of the press campaign and the lurid headlines and pictures which implied that the Wehrmacht would be marching down Whitehall, warned Germans not to underestimate 'the plain nastiness of a large part of the British press'. However, most of those who spoke also stressed the common ground between Britain and Germany and proposed positive action to help create a better climate of opinion. Theo Sommer summed it up by saying: 'When it comes to Anglo-German relations, we have been fighting phantom battles. Far too frequently we fail to stress where we see eye to eye.'

The extent of the economic interdependence between the two countries is very striking. In 1993, Germany was Britain's largest single trading partner, with 14 per cent of the import/export total: British exports to Germany totalled DM 33,163 million, while German exports to Britain, at DM 46,614 million, were over a third more. Britain is somewhat less important in terms of trade to Germany but is still one of the leading trading partners, with 6.9 per cent of total trade; it also provides the fourth largest German export market. Germany is one of the largest investors in Britain – 1,000 German firms are located here, creating 100,000 direct jobs and 120,000 indirect ones. Britain is also a substantial investor in Germany, including the eastern

Länder. This economic interdependence means that firms have become increasingly reliant on each other's markets – Britons and Germans work in each other's countries, while consumers became used to buying each other's goods. So a stable and prosperous Germany becomes a British interest, and a stable and prosperous Britain becomes a German interest.

Both Britain and Germany are key members of the European Union. While conflicting attitudes on European integration have caused problems in the past, and may do so again in the future, there are strong underlying common interests. The most obvious, rising from their common position as important trading nations, is their shared commitment to open markets, as shown by the close alliance the two countries formed during the GATT negotiations in 1993. Though from a different perspective, both countries strongly support the widening of the EU to its east, by bringing in Poland, Hungary, the Czech Republic and Slovakia as members. It is essential for Europe's future that Germany should continue to have close relations with France but, in the future, it may need the support of Britain more than it did before unification and the end of the Cold War. Provided Britain can develop a more positive view of its European role, a close relationship with Britain could supplement the existing Franco-German alliance. In the view of a leading German foreign affairs specialist, 'an active triangle' between Germany, France and Britain would not only lessen Germany's political dependence on France but also give a better balance to the European Community.

The British and the Germans have extremely close defence links. In contrast to France, both countries are full members of NATO and have been allies for forty years. The British still have over 20,000 troops on German soil. Many German army, navy and air force officers have been trained in Britain. There are personal ties developed over many years. Klaus Naumann, Chief of Staff of the Bundeswehr, told me that, despite the Franco-German corps, the German military have better links with their British counterparts. In the late 1990s, following the endorsement by the German Constitutional Court of the legality of German involvement in peace-keeping military missions abroad, German forces will need to become more flexible. They will need British assistance. They are already involved with Britain in NATO's air mobile division. And, as the United States cuts back its forces on the European mainland, Britain's participation in NATO and in the Western European Union will assume greater importance for the Germans, especially with such an unstable area to their east. A German air force colonel said to me: 'We really need British help and support.'

More fundamentally, both Britain and Germany are western democracies which share a commitment to democratic institutions, free markets and to the welfare state. Mr Kohl's Christian Democrat-led coalition may give a higher priority to the social dimension than Mr Major's Conservative Government. The German political system may be more decentralized, rights-based and consensus-orientated than the British one. But, even if these differences in values and attitudes lead to disagreement in European debates, the two countries share similar problems. They are both trying to improve competitiveness, while maintaining social cohesion. They both have similar domestic priorities, including reducing unemployment, tackling crime, making education more effective, coping with environmental pollution, and weathering social security strains. Both countries could learn from each other's successes – and failures too. If many British observers rightly admire German productivity, the high level of skills, the federal structure and the capacity to tackle difficult problems within a framework of political and social consensus, some Germans also think that their country could benefit from the invigorating British experience of inward investment and an efficient service sector.

In an interview with the London *Times*, on the eve of an Anglo-German summit in November 1993, Klaus Kinkel, the German Foreign Minister, was depicted as plundering the thesaurus to depict the relationship with London: 'Unspectacular, a quiet alliance . . . open . . . friendly . . . solid . . . dependable . . . professional'. *The Times*'s correspondent commented that Kinkel might have been describing his dentist. Given the joint experience, overlapping interests and the common problems which both countries now share, something a little warmer than the dentist/patient relationship is now required. Positive and sustained steps should be taken to strengthen the Anglo-German understanding.

The main priority is to improve the knowledge of each other's country. Germans, while respecting their commitment to democracy and 'fair play', tend to see the British as 'backward looking' and insular, and, as far as Europe is concerned, 'untrustworthy'. Asked to give three British character traits, a straw poll of German students said 'conservative' and 'traditional'. In 1993, Hans Klein, then vice-president of the Bundestag, said to me, 'It is about time that two of Europe's most important nations got to know each other.' And as a leader in the *Financial Times* in April 1994 pointed out, 'There is a special need to counter ignorance among ordinary British people about life in modern Germany.' Lack of knowledge allows prejudice to gain hold and, as opinion polls show, generates distrust. It is important to expand existing schemes of educational and youth exchanges, which are too small and without sufficient financial backing, especially on the British side. What is required is a mass programme of exchanges on the Franco-

German model. Ten times more is spent on Franco-German exchanges than on Anglo-German ones. German language teaching should be dramatically stepped up in British schools, as should the number of German study courses, including history and politics, at British universities. 'Catch them young,' should be the watchword.

Town twinning with German towns and cities should be increased. Having links, as does my constituency, with towns in the Ruhr not only gives councillors the opportunity to meet their opposite numbers but, more important, provides an umbrella for a wide range of cultural, sporting and educational exchanges. The sign under a British town's name post that it is twinned with a German town – or *vice versa* – is also an important symbol of Anglo-German friendship.

Biased anti-German reporting in the British tabloid press should be firmly counteracted by British-German friendship and liaison groups, which should in any case be taking a more pro-active role in putting over an objective and up to date view of what is happening in Germany. Business, which depends so greatly on the German market, ought to be making a much greater contribution to ensuring that there is more awareness of Germany in this country. Trade unions, voluntary organizations and the political parties should be expanding joint programmes with their opposite numbers in Germany.

The British Government has a special responsibility for the improvement of Anglo-German relations. It is really about time that British political leaders started paying tribute to Germany's post-war success, especially to the establishment and development of democratic institutions and freedoms in the Federal Republic. They should also recognize publicly the immense effort which Germany, following unification, is making to transform the eastern part of the country. Above all, they should explain clearly to their countrymen that a strong and democratic Germany, linked, as it is, to other countries by a number of treaties and institutions, especially the European Union and NATO, is greatly in Britain's and Europe's interest.

A close relationship is very much to the advantage of Britain and Germany. Together with France, these two countries are the key members of the European Union. Working together, they can not only help each other but also provide a force for progress and stability throughout the Continent. The time has come for a major drive to improve the Anglo-German relationship.

## Conclusion

## THE FUTURE OF THE GERMANS

'With unification in 1990 a united Germany has emerged
that has never existed in history before: a steadfast
democracy without territorial claims and without foes.
A nation that with her values, political institutions, her
economic survival and her foreign policy is deeply
interwoven with the West – especially Western
Europe.'

*Karl Kaiser*[1]

'Whoever thinks about Germany now, and seeks answers for the German question, must include Auschwitz
in his thoughts.'

*Günter Grass*[2]

Sunday 16 October 1994, the day on which Germany
voted, was fine and sunny. In Bonn, there was a nip in the
air and the trees had turned red and gold. At about 5.30
p.m., I went to Erich Ollenhauer House, the Social Democrat headquarters, for their election party. The mood was
downbeat. After the European elections in June when the
CDU/CSU had finished comfortably ahead and after an
uncertain campaign, SPD supporters were expecting to
lose. But the first TV prediction just after 6 p.m. indicated
a close result. A murmur went round the hall. It looked as
though the SPD had polled nearly 37 per cent, over 4
per cent higher than at the European elections in June and
3 per cent higher than at the 1990 elections. The CDU/
CSU were ahead at 41.5 per cent, but their share of the
poll was 2 per cent down on 1990 and well short of an
overall majority.

The key lay with the smaller parties. The Greens, who

had campaigned hard for a Red-Green coalition, were back in parliament with over 7 per cent, but so were Chancellor Kohl's coalition ally, the FDP, with 6.9 per cent. SPD strategists told me that, in normal circumstances, that would have been enough for a Kohl victory. The cause of uncertainty was the PDS, the successor to the East German Communist Party. Although they were short of the 5 per cent overall figure needed to get into the Bundestag, it seemed as though they had polled so well in East Berlin that they would win the three individual mandates necessary to get in to parliament by the alternative route. When there was a news flash that the Communist candidate, Stefan Heym, had won in Berlin, a cheer rang out, even though the beaten candidate was the Social Democrat Wolfgang Thierse, and the SPD had competed fiercely with the PDS for votes in the East. For just a moment, they allowed themselves to believe that the Chancellor might not have a majority after all.

Helmut Kohl knew otherwise. Showing all his old will to power, he appeared confidently on television to claim victory and predicted 'a perfectly good working majority' for the coalition. Kohl was right, at least in the short term. When all the results had been counted, the outgoing coalition had appeared to have an overall majority of ten – wafer thin but enough.

The FDP leader and Foreign Minister, Klaus Kinkel, did not bother to disguise his relief. After a series of disastrous Länder elections when his party failed to be returned to regional parliaments, the FDP's 6.9 per cent could be presented as a triumph. But, as Kinkel said that night, it had been a 'tough fight'. The FDP had only survived thanks to CDU 'second votes'. In German elections, the first vote is for the individual candidate, the second is for the party list and mainly determines the share of the seats. Exit polls showed that nearly two thirds of FDP supporters preferred the CDU. With only minimal regional success, the FDP was now more dependent than ever on the CDU for survival, hardly a healthy situation for an independent party.

Rudolf Scharping, the SPD Chancellor candidate, looked far happier after the result than he had all summer. Gone was the stiffness and inner tension. Seemingly relaxed and confident, he told TV interviewers that the new Government would be 'a coalition of losers' and that the SPD was in 'a very strong position'. On the face of it, this seemed a paradoxical claim. After all, at the beginning of the year he had been riding high in the public opinion polls and Kohl had seemed to be heading for retirement. Yet Scharping had a point. The SPD had improved its position in the Bundestag and, after its impressive showing in most of the 1994 Länder elections, had strengthened its hold over the Bundesrat. If Kohl wanted to get his legislation through, he would have to consult the SPD. On the day after the election, Thomas Meyer of the Frankfurt office of the American investment bank Goldman Sachs, wrote prophetically 'Germany will be ruled by a *defacto* grand coalition in effect'.[3]

A month after the election, on Tuesday 15 November, following coalition talks between the CDU, the CSU and the FDP, Helmut Kohl was re-elected Chancellor by one vote more than the absolute majority of 337 he needed. One of the votes was his own. Another was that of a white faced Roland Richter, a new CDU deputy, who arrived in the Bundestag only two minutes before voting ended, after being hauled out of his hotel bed.

Kohl shrugged off the narrowness of his victory, pointing out that Konrad Adenauer had been elected in 1949 with the bare minimum, while Helmut Schmidt had only one vote to spare in 1976. Once in, German Chancellors are hard to get out. There are no by-elections in the

German system, deputies being replaced off the party lists, and, to win a no-confidence vote, the opposition needs an absolute majority for a candidate of its own.

However, there were warning signals for the Chancellor. In a second ballot, three members of the coalition parties, probably Free Democrats, voted against Kohl. As a CDU deputy pointed out to me, in the 1994 Bundestag, in contrast to the 1990 Bundestag, there is a potential alternative majority – a so-called 'traffic light' coalition of the SPD, the FDP and the Greens. The electoral weakness of the FDP means that, in order to survive as a party, it may need, sooner rather than later, to detach itself from the CDU, especially if the Chancellor decides to leave office before the next federal election in 1998.

Yet, despite the closeness of the result, the 1994 Federal election revealed a greater political stability in Germany than commentators had imagined possible two years earlier. The party of the right-wing extremists, the Republican Party, which in April 1992 had won 10.9 per cent in the Baden-Württemberg Land election, received only 1.9 per cent of the all-German vote, a catastrophic performance. The two major parties – the CDU-CSU and the SPD – between them won nearly 78 per cent of the vote, while the four main democratic parties – the CDU-CSU, the SPD, the FDP and the Greens – polled between them more than 92 per cent.

The only disturbing note of the 1994 election was the impressive performance of the PDS in East Germany. While the PDS won only 4.4 per cent in Germany overall, it gained almost 20 per cent and more than 1.7 million votes in the East. Though it undoubtedly benefited from the attacks made on it during the election by Chancellor Kohl, its most powerful argument was that it represented the interests of the East Germans. The PDS's strength is a clear demonstration of Eastern discontent and also indicates how far Germany has to go before East and West can be said to be fully united.

The March 1990 Chequers Memorandum (see p. 102) asked the tactless but still crucial question: could democracy in Germany survive a major setback? My answer, based on the vigour of the Federal Republic's institutions, the support of Germans for these institutions, and on how the country has coped with the twin tests of recession and restructuring since unification, is 'yes'.

Democracy is firmly rooted in Germany. Drawing on American and British experience and advice, playing to German strengths and, above all, learning the lessons of the past, the founding fathers devised a set of democratic institutions and rules which have, over forty years, proved their resilience. The federal structure, encouraged by the Americans but firmly based on German tradition, maintains a balance between national decision making and the regional autonomy and variety so characteristic of Germany. The mixture of proportional representation tempered by the 5 per cent hurdle, strong democratic political parties and the prominent position of the Chancellor ensures that effective government is combined with a wide measure of political consensus. The 'social market' institutions introduce a degree of consensus into economic and industrial decision making. Two prestigious bodies act as guardians: the Federal Constitutional Court at Karlsruhe watches over the democratic constitution, while the Bundesbank protects the Deutsche Mark, the symbol of German post-war success. The Federal Republic, now extended eastwards through unification, has been the most successful regime in German history – 'Civic, civilian and civilized', as Timothy Garton Ash has called it.

The British, who made an important contribution to German democracy by helping establish the German electoral system, by insisting on a non-political civil service and by advising that German trade unions should be set up on an industrial basis, could now take lessons from the Germans. It is not a question of a direct export of institutions from one country to another. The Bundesbank is, for example, a peculiarly German institution set up because of German experience. There is, however, a case for a more autonomous Bank of England, operationally responsible for monetary policy. British employers could learn from the commitment of German industry to social partnership and to education and training. British politicians, working in a highly conflictual and centralized system, should consider the advantages of German federalism, the electoral system and the consensual method of government, so characteristic of the Federal Republic.

If Weimar was a democracy without democrats, Bonn has demonstrated itself to be a democracy with the support of an overwhelming majority of its citizens. In contrast to Weimar, all its political leaders, most of whom have been of outstanding quality, have been strongly committed to democracy. Again in contrast to Weimar, its élites, its business leaders, its military, its civil servants, its cultural intelligentsia, its media and opinion formers all support the Federal Republic. The democratic parties are strong, while extremist parties, whether of right or left, have received little consistent support, with the exception of the PDS in East Germany (and there are special reasons for that). As in both Britain and France, there has been a totally unacceptable level of racist violence in the 1990s. But the response of German democrats has been at least as impressive as their British and French counterparts − the huge candlelight demonstrations, the new policing and protective measures, and the banning of neo-Nazi organizations. The young generation (though, as the rise of the Greens has demonstrated, critical of some aspects of modern life), is arguably even more committed to democracy than its predecessors. So the omens look good for German democracy.

Furthermore, at the same time as proving its democratic credentials, Germany has shown itself to be a good neighbour. From Adenauer's *Westpolitik* onwards, the Federal Republic has become ever more closely linked to the West. It is a key member of NATO and a founder member of the European Union. Its post-war alliance with France has been the driving force behind European Union. Its trade is overwhelmingly with its European partners and the United States. On the other hand, through Brandt's *Ostpolitik* it has made peace with its Eastern neighbours – with the old Soviet Union, and with Poland, Hungary and the former Czechoslovakia. The new unity of a Germany firmly tied to the West but also with no enemies and no territorial claims to the East has been peacefully if cautiously accepted by its European neighbours.

The prospects for a larger, potentially more powerful Germany living at peace are promising. Learning from the past, the Germans, as opinion polls show, are amongst the least militaristic people in Europe. As the historian Gordon A. Craig puts it:

> Having returned after the catastrophe of 1945 to the theory of individual rights and the principles of the Enlightenment and western liberalism, they have become accustomed to moving with, rather than against, the tide of European civilization, and they seem determined this time to be a reliable part of the European order.[4]

The united Germany, however, faces severe challenges in the next five years which will test both its resolve and its institutions.

The most obvious is unifying West and East Germany. The problems of bringing together the Germans of the old Federal Republic with the Germans of the former GDR were grossly underestimated by Chancellor Kohl's coalition. Glaring errors were made, especially the 1 to 1 exchange rate. The collapse of East German industry was a traumatic experience, leading to prolonged unemployment and widespread disruption. The gulf between *Wessis* and *Ossis* is still very wide. According to polls, only a small minority of both parts feel themselves to be one people.

Yet, despite the initial over-optimism and errors of policy, there is a strong probability that the German people will in time achieve a genuine unification of East and West. The adoption by the East of the Federal Basic Law provides a common constitutional and legal framework, and Federal social welfare underpins living conditions in the East. The sustained Federal investment in basic infra-structure, especially in up-to-date transport and communica-tions systems, is likely to pay off in new industrial investment.

Already, there is a big expansion of the service sector in the East. Provided that there is a steady economic expansion in the West and that German taxpayers continue to under-write the new Länder, then, probably towards the end of the decade, the East German economy will begin a process of self-sustaining growth. There *will* be 'blooming land-scapes', if much later than Chancellor Kohl promised. Bringing the two parts of Germany socially and psychologi-cally closer together will take much longer. But, when it becomes clearer that there is a real economic improvement in the East and the cost of unification is declining for the West, then pride of achievement is likely to serve as a unifying factor.

Much will depend on the successful restructuring of the West German economy. The question is whether the 'social market' system will prove flexible enough to enable Germany to re-equip and modernize. In 1992–93, most of the big German firms moved decisively to bring their costs back into line. But there is much more to be done, including speeding up innovation, reforming higher education, and training, and creating greater flexibility in the labour market, especially in the service sector. However, the 'social market' institutions, especially the partnership between capital and labour in the 'stakeholder' company, provide a mechanism which should enable the German economy to respond to global change, while maintaining social cohesion.

The well-established German commitment to consensus will almost certainly ensure that these twin transformations – unification and restructuring – are carried through within the same constitutional framework that has served Germany so well over the last four decades. The underlying stability of the system was demonstrated by the result of the 1994 election, in which the democratic parties got over 90 per cent of the vote and, even in East Germany, 80 per cent of the electorate voted for the established parties, although the big vote for the PDS there is a warning against complacency. If sometimes political change comes slowly in Germany, as over the asylum laws and financing public spending in the East, change is often surer and more lasting than in other parliamentary democracies. All the same, the determination and courage of German democratic politicians is likely to be severely tested in the second half of the 1990s.

In foreign policy, there are difficult choices to be made and delicate balances to be struck. Chancellor Kohl, like his predecessors and his likely successors, remains firmly committed to the West and its multilateral institutions, especially NATO and the European Union. With respect to the EU, there is a strong case, which has been argued by its main European partner, France, for further integration, especially for monetary union and a single currency. Yet there is overwhelming German opposition, as shown by the polls, to giving up the D-Mark. And, as Volker Rühe has strongly hinted, there is at least some tension between integrating further with Germany's Western partners and extending the European Union further East.

It must be a top German priority to create a zone of stability on its Eastern borders. The uncertain future of Russia, the near anarchy of other parts of the old Soviet Union, and the power vacuum in Eastern Europe make it all the more essential to build up a group of prosperous, democratic countries like Poland, Hungary, the Czech Republic and Slovakia. But Germany cannot afford, either economically or politically, to act by itself. And, though the 'reform' democracies of Eastern Europe seek German support, it is the multilateral institutions of Western Europe, above all NATO and the EU, which can provide the kind of guarantees which these countries seek. The problem for Germany is to persuade its partners, above all France, of the importance of an early opening of the European Union to the East.

German politicians will also have the task of persuading their own people, especially the younger generation, that, in the post-Cold War world, being an important member of NATO and a candidate for permanent membership of the UN Security Council, requires an 'out of area' military contribution. Keeping the peace may involve force. If the Bosnia tragedy has shown anything, it is that speedy and decisive use of military power may often be necessary if peace is to be preserved. Germany can no longer opt out.

The Chequers Memorandum of 1990 summarized a whole list of unflattering German attitudes (see p.190) from which Mrs Thatcher, when she came to write her memoirs, chose two – 'angst' and 'aggressiveness' – to sum up the German national character. But how legitimate is it to make generalizations about whole nations? Theodor Zeldin, in his brilliant study of the French, puts the dilemma succinctly: 'To describe a nation of 54 million, still less one of 220 million, in a single phrase . . . is a natural reaction in the face of the complexity of the world, but it is a habit born of despair, which persists because there seems no obvious way of avoiding it'.[5] In the case of the Germans, the sharp regional distinctions between northerners and Bavarians, between Catholic Bavarians and Protestant Swabians, between Rhinelanders and Westphalians, between Saxons and Mecklenburgers, and between Berliners and the rest, make generalizations about national stereotypes even more hazardous.

There is an additional problem. Most of the well known descriptions of Germany and the Germans are drawn from the past, either from the period before the first German unification or from the seventy-five troubled years following it. We have the early nineteenth-century German poet Heinrich Heine declaring gloomily in his *Deutschland, ein Wintermärchen* (published in 1844), 'When I think of Germany in the night, I am robbed of my sleep', and in 1886 Friedrich Nietzsche, the German philosopher, writing in *Beyond Good or Evil*, said that it was characteristic of the Germans 'that one is seldom wholly wrong about them. The German soul has corridors and interconnecting corridors in it, there are caves, hiding places, dungeons in it, its disorder possesses much of the fascinating and mysterious, the German is acquainted with the hidden paths to chaos.' In the 1930s, de Gaulle said something similar when he described Germany as 'a sublime but glaucous sea where the fisherman's net hauls up monsters and treasures'.[6]

On the other hand, Madame de Staël, in her *De l'Allemagne* published at the beginning of the nineteenth century, painted an attractive picture of a land of philosophers, poets and peasants – '*la patrie de la pensée*' she called it. So far from being militaristic, she described Germans as peace loving – even their soldiers were slow and timid. The very different idea of Germany and the Germans portrayed by Madame de Staël suggests that what are sometimes put forward as the abiding characteristics of a people in reality change with time and circumstance.

Today's Germans are very different from the Germans of the later nineteenth and early twentieth century or the Germans of the 1930s and early 1940s. They are proven democrats, committed over many years to consensus and peace. They have developed strong democratic institutions which have been much tested, especially in the traumatic years of change since unification. Risking a generalization, if the Germans have a fault, it is that they do not take enough pride in their achievements and do not have enough confidence in their ability to surmount difficulties in the future, even if some of these difficulties, especially bringing together East and West, are big ones.

I have sometimes heard Germans, particularly since unification, ask questions about their own identity in a way which neither the British nor the French ever would. In a celebrated essay 'What does it mean to be German', Richard von Weizsäcker, former German president, wrote:

> The Germans, in my opinion, have a different and often a more strained relation to the act of providing or creating form than, for example, our Latin neighbours ... With us, an achieved form has an immediate tendency to become a problem.[7]

It is of course understandable, given the horrors of the past, the different post-war experiences of the two parts of Germany and now their dramatic coming together in a nation state, that the issue of German identity should be raised anew. It will, in any case, take time for a genuine feeling of community between East and West to develop. Michael Mertes, head of Chancellor Kohl's policy unit, suggests that the challenge for the Germans is

> to develop a calm patriotism based not only on their indivisible history (not excluding its darker chapters), their common cultural

traditions, but also, and most importantly, on shared democratic values, civil responsibility for their own *respublica*, an active sense of solidarity and togetherness.[8]

Yet their political and economic progress over the last four decades ought to give the Germans confidence that the problems of national unification and industrial regeneration can be successfully overcome. What has already been achieved since 1990 should also act as an encouragement. It may be the case that the 'most difficult but also quintessential task before the Germans and their intellectual and political leaders today is very simply to manage united Germany with self-confidence'.[9] But, given their impressive record since 1945, there is every reason why the Germans should have confidence in themselves and in their future.

It is vital for the whole of Europe that Germany is successful in uniting its Eastern and its Western parts economically, socially and psychologically. A successful unification will remove one of Europe's most troublesome flashpoints on a permanent basis. It will demonstrate that it is possible to transform a Communist command economy into a market system, provided that there is consistent investment and support. And it will greatly strengthen the German economy.

A strong and expanding German economy, hopefully made more efficient by further restructuring, is good for the rest of Europe. The German economy is the motor of Europe. Its health is, therefore, essential for the economies of its partners, including Britain, whose top trading partner is Germany.

Germany has a key role to play as a team leader in the European Union. Because of its power and geographical position, it is inevitably the European Union's lead player in Eastern Europe. If the task of the last forty years has been to bring together the formerly warring 'nations' of

Western Europe, the priority of the next decade will be bringing Central and Eastern European countries like Poland, Hungary and the Czech Republic into the European Community and NATO.

A confident European Germany, tied to its partners by trade, treaty and integration, is crucial for the dynamism and direction of the European Community. It would be bad for Europe if Germany was so bowed down by its internal problems or by its past history that it did not feel able to pull its weight in Europe. It is in European and British interests for a democratic Germany to be politically strong and economically successful. The British, in particular, need to recognize the importance of Germany to them and seek a closer partnership.

Germans should never forget the past. But they should also take legitimate pride in their impressive post-war achievements and accept their new responsibilities, in the uncertain post-Cold War world, as the biggest and most powerful member of the European Union.

# Notes

Introduction: THE GERMANS AS THEY ARE

1. Martin Gilbert, *Winston Churchill: Road to Victory*, Heinemann, London, 1990, p.1344
2. Timothy Garton Ash, *We the People*, London, 1990, p.63
3. Quoted in David Marsh, *Germany and Europe*, Heinemann, London, 1994, p.47
4. *The Independent*, 1 March 1993
5. Poll data in the *Guardian*, December 1990
6. *Guardian*, April 1994
7. Richard von Weizsäcker, *A Voice From Germany*, Weidenfeld & Nicolson, London, 1986, p.48
8. Quoted in Alan Bullock, *Hitler and Stalin*, Fontana, London, 1993, pp.1056–1057
9. A.J.P. Taylor, *The Course of German History*, University Paperbacks, London, 1961, p.11
10. Richard J. Evans, *In Hitler's Shadow*, Pantheon Books, New York, 1988, pp.103–104
11. Richard J. Evans, op. cit., particularly chapters 1 and 6
12. Gordon A. Craig, *The Germans*, Penguin Books, London, 1991, p.26
13. Noel Annan, *Portrait of a Generation*, Weidenfeld & Nicolson, London, 1990, p.248

Chapter One: ONE PEOPLE: TWO HISTORIES

1. Elizabeth Pond, *Beyond the Wall*, Brookings, New York, 1993, p.20
2. Quoted in Timothy Garton Ash, *In Europe's Name*, Cape, London, 1993, p.344
3. Anne McElvoy, *The Saddled Cow*, Faber & Faber, London, 1993, pp.201–202
4. Timothy Garton Ash, *We the People*, Granta Books, Cambridge, p.62
5. Anne McElvoy, op. cit., p.208
6. Mary Fulbrook, *The Divided Nation*, Fontana, London, p.335
7. Elizabeth Pond, op. cit., p.172

8. Willy Brandt, *My Life in Politics*, Penguin, London, 1993, p.xix
9. Timothy Garton Ash, op. cit., p.10
10. John Ardagh, *Germany and the Germans*, Penguin, London, 1991, p.439
11. Timothy Garton Ash, op. cit., p.196
12. Peter Schneider, *The German Comedy*, I.B. Tauris, London, 1992, p.13

Chapter Three: WESTERN RESENTMENT: PAYING THROUGH THE NOSE

1. Quoted in David Marsh, *The Bundesbank*, Heinemann, London, 1992, p.212
2. *Deutsch-English Gespräch*, Königswinter conference, 25–27 March 1993, p.9
3. David Marsh, op. cit., p.213
4. Quoted in Alan Watson, *The Germans*, Mandarin, London, 1994, p.398
5. Helmut Schmidt, *Handeln für Deutschland*, Rowohlt, 1993
6. *Der Spiegel*, August 1994, p.43
7. IFO Digest, IFO Institute, Munich, February 1994

Chapter Four: TRIBAL GERMANY: THE STRENGTHS OF FEDERALISM

1. Thomas Kielinger, 'Sixteen Tribes of Germany' in *Meet United Germany: Perspectives 1992–93, Frankfurter Allgemeine Zeitung*, 1992, p.55
2. John Ardagh, op. cit., p.85
3. *The Economist*, 'Model Vision', 21 May 1994, p.29
4. Charles Handy, *The Empty Raincoat*, Hutchinson, London, 1994, p.102
5. Norman Stone, *The Sunday Times*, 29 November 1992
6. Golo Mann, *The History of Germany Since 1789*, Penguin, London, 1990, p.83
7. Berlin: Bonn *Die Debatte*, Verlag Kiepenhauer und Witsch, 1991
8. Quoted in Alan Watson, op. cit., p.2
9. Anthony Read and David Fisher, *Berlin*, Pimlico, London, 1994, p.317
10. Quoted in Alan Watson, op. cit., p.211

Chapter Five: THE FATHERS OF THE REPUBLIC

1. Terence Prittie, *The Velvet Chancellors*, Frederick Muller, London, 1979, p.252

2. Lewis J. Edwiger, *Politics in West Germany*, Boston, 1977; quoted in Gordon A. Craig, op. cit., p.44

3. Willy Brandt, op. cit., p.27

4. Golo Mann, op. cit., p.834

5. Gordon A. Craig, op. cit., p.44

6. Willy Brandt, op. cit., p.30

7. Paul Weymar, *Adenauer*, André Deutsch, London, 1957, p.348

8. Charles Wighton, *Adenauer – Democratic Dictator*, Muller, London, 1963

9. Paul Weyman, op. cit., p.516

10. Ibid., p.523

11. Willy Brandt, *People and Politics*, London, 1978

12. Terence Prittie, op. cit., p.116

13. Quoted in Alan Watson, op. cit., p.235

14. Gordon A. Craig, op. cit., p.43

15. Quoted in David Marsh, *The Germans*, Century Hutchinson, London, 1989, p.86

16. Willy Brandt, op. cit.

17. Günter Grass

18. Quoted in Terence Prittie, op. cit.

19. Willy Brandt, *My Life in Politics*, p.1

20. Willy Brandt, *People and Politics*, p.20

21. Ibid.

22. H. Becker, *Auf dem Weg zur lernenden Gesellschaft*, Stuttgart, 1980, p.6

23. Willy Brandt, *My Life in Politics*, pp.296–297

24. Quoted in Gordon A. Craig, op. cit., p.59

25. Willy Brandt, op. cit., p.200

26. Denis Healey in *The Independent Magazine*, 17 October 1992

27. Much of what follows, including quotations, is drawn from Jonathan Carr, *Helmut Schmidt*, Weidenfeld & Nicolson, London, 1985

28. Karl Kaiser, 'Schmidt's Foreign Policy', *New York Times*, 21 January 1979

29. Quoted in a specially rewritten last chapter for a new German edition of Jonathan Carr's *Helmut Schmidt*

30. Elizabeth Pond, *Beyond the Wall*, Brookings, Washington, 1993, p.62


Chapter Six: DEMOCRATS AND EXTREMISTS

1. Gordon Smith, *Democracy in Western Germany*, Dartmouth, London, 1990, p.47
2. Mary Fulbrook, *Germany 1918–1900*, Fontana, London, 1991, pp.31–32
3. Gordon Smith, op. cit., p.66
4. Ibid., p.92
5. Peter Pulzer, 'Political Parties and Democracy' in *Meet United Germany, Frankfurter Allgemeine Zeitung*, 1992, p.70
6. Willy Brandt, op. cit., p.76
7. Peter Pulzer, op. cit., p.70
8. Golo Mann, op. cit., p.808
9. Willy Brandt, op. cit., p.28
10. Alan Watson, op. cit., p.356
11. Peter Pulzer, op. cit., p.78
12. Alan Watson, op. cit., pp.213–214


Chapter Seven: THE D-MARK AND THE BUNDESBANK

1. David Marsh, *The Bundesbank*, p.10. I have drawn on this excellent account for some of the background to this chapter
2. Quoted in David Marsh, op. cit., p.250
3. Alan Bullock, *Hitler*, Pelican, London, 1967, pp.90–91
4. Quoted in Gordon A. Craig, op. cit., p.123
5. David Marsh, op. cit.
6. Ibid., p.170
7. Ibid., p.71
8. David Marsh, *Germany and Europe*, Heinemann, London, 1994, p.74
9. David Marsh, *The Bundesbank*, p.216
10. Ibid., p.218
11. David Marsh, *Germany and Europe*, p.147
12. Ibid., p.161
13. Ibid., p.141

Chapter Eight: THE SOCIAL MARKET ECONOMY: CAN IT SURVIVE?

1. David Goodhart, *The Reshaping of the German Social Market*, Institute for Public Research, London, 1994, p.3. I have used this valuable work in preparing this chapter

2. Ibid., p.7

3. Ibid., p.21

4. Charles Handy, *The Empty Raincoat*, Hutchinson, London, 1994, p.155–156.

5. Bert Clough in *College Management Today*

6. David Goodhart, op. cit., p.13

7. *The Economist*, 'Model Vision', 21 May 1994

8. Alan Watson, op. cit., p.186

9. Quoted in David Marsh, op. cit., p. 107

10. Ibid., pp.120–121

11. *Herald Tribune*, 3 March 1993

12. *Financial Times*, 21 December 1993

13. Kurt J. Lauk's 'Germany at the Crossroads' in *Germany in Transition*, Daedalus, Cambridge MA, Winter 1994, p.78

14. IFO Digest, June 1994, p.18

15. *The Economist*, 'Model Vision'

16. *Financial Times*, 12 April 1994

17. *Financial Times*, 24 September 1994

18. Kurt J. Lauk, 'Germany at the Crossroads,' p. 73

19. *Financial Times*, 9 November 1993

20. *The Economist*, 6 March 1993

21. Charles Handy, *The Empty Raincoat*, p.156

22. David Goodhart, op. cit., p.50

23. Ibid., p.50

Chapter Nine: GERMAN INTELLECTUALS AND DEMOCRACY

1. Gordon A. Craig, op. cit., p.30

2. Richard Friedenthal, *Goethe*, Weidenfeld & Nicolson, London, 1989, p.428

3. Quoted in Ralf Dahrendorf, *Society and Democracy in Germany*, Weidenfeld & Nicolson, London, 1965, p.285

4. Karl Popper, *The Open Society and its Enemies*, Routledge and Kegan Paul, London, 1957, Volume 2, p.30

5. Gordon A. Craig, op. cit., p.33

6. John Ardagh, op. cit., p.303

7. *Der Spiegel*, 3 July 1994
8. *The Times*, 6 October 1994
9. *The Economist*, 12 March 1994

Chapter Ten: GERMANY'S ROLE IN THE WORLD: GOOD PARTNER OR 'SPECIAL WAY'?

1. Hans-Peter Schwarz, 'Germany's National and European Interests' in *Germany's New Position in Europe*, edited Arnulf Baring Berg, Oxford/Providence, 1994, p.117
2. Timothy Garton Ash, 'Germany's Choice', *Foreign Affairs*, July/August 1994, p.79
3. Godfrey Hodgson in *The Independent*, 13 November 1994
4. Thomas Kielinger and Max Otto, 'Germany: The Pressured Power', in *Foreign Policy*, Summer 1993
5. Timothy Garton Ash, 'Germany's Choice', op. cit., p.67
6. *The Economist*, 20 November 1993
7. Timothy Garton Ash, op. cit., p.69
8. *The Independent*, 18 October 1994
9. *Financial Times*, 3 November 1993
10. Arnulf Baring in *Germany's New Position in Europe*, p.15
11. A.J.P. Taylor, *The Course of German History*, Methuen, London, 1961, p.2
12. Timothy Garton Ash, *In Europe's Name*, Jonathan Cape, London, 1993, pp.279–280
13. Jochen Thies in *Germany's New Position in Europe*, pp.73–74
14. Timothy Garton Ash, op. cit., p.403

Chapter Eleven: BRITAIN AND GERMANY: THE OPPORTUNITY FOR PARTNERSHIP

1. Anthony Glees, 'The Diplomacy of Anglo-German relations', *German Politics*, Vol.13, No.1, p.76
2. Paul Kennedy, *The Rise of the Anglo-German Antagonism*, Allen & Unwin, London, 1980, p.41
3. Ibid., p.121
4. Rosemary Ashton, *The German Idea*, Cambridge University Press, Cambridge, 1980
5. Raymond Sontag, *Germany and England 1848–1894*, Appleton Century, New York, 1938, p.325

6. 'Memorandum by Eyre Crowe', *British Documents* on the origins of the war 1898–1914, Vol.III, p.405, HMSO, London, 1928

7. Quoted in A.J. Mardor, *From The Dreadnought to Scapa Flow*, Vol.1, Oxford University Press, Oxford, 1961, p.322

8. Quoted in David Calleo, *The German Problem Reconsidered*, Cambride University Press, Cambridge, 1978, p.33

9. George Orwell, *The Lion and the Unicorn*, Penguin Books, Harmondsworth, p.49

10. Golo Mann, *The History of Germany since 1789*, Penguin Books, Harmondsworth, 1990, p.689

11. Christabel Bielenberg, *The Past is Myself*, Corgi, London, 1987, pp.45–46

12. Timothy Garton Ash, *The Times*, 20 October 1994

13. Margaret Thatcher, *The Downing Street Years*, Harper Collins, London, 1993, p.796

14. 'What the Prime Minister learnt about the Germans', *The Independent on Sunday*, 15 July 1990

15. Margaret Thatcher, *The Downing Street Years*, p.312

16. 'Saying the Unsayable about the Germans', *Spectator*, 14 July 1990

17. *Guardian*, 3 May 1993

18. *The Economist*, 18 January 1992

19. Kenan Malik, 'A Britain still at war with Germany', *The Independent*, 16 June 1994

20. Valerie Steward, *German Foreign Policy Challenges After Unification*, Wilton Park Paper, November 1993

21. James Fenton, *The Independent*, 1 March 1993

Conclusion: THE FUTURE OF THE GERMANS

1. Karl Kaiser *Das vereinigte Deutschland in der internationalen Politik*, Karl Kaiser und Hans W. Maul (ed.), *Deutschlands neue Aussenpolitik* Band 1: Grundlagen, Oldenbourg Verlag, Muenchen, 1994, p.2

2. Günter Grass 'On Loss' in *The Future of German Democracy*, Robert Gerald Livingston and Volkmar Sandor, Continuan, New York, 1993, p.150

3. *German Economic Commentary*, Goldman Sachs, Frankfurt, 17 October 1994

4. Gordon A. Craig, op. cit., p.320

5. Theodore Zeldin, *The French*, Collins Harvill, London, 1988, p.509

6. Quoted in John Newhouse, *De Gaulle and the Anglo-Saxons* André Deutsch, London, 1970

7. Richard von Weizsäcker, *A Voice from Germany*, Weidenfield & Nicolson, London, 1986

8. Michael Mertes, 'Germany's Social and Political Culture' in *Germany in Transition*, Cambridge MA, Daedalus, Winter 1994, p.23

9. Steven Muller, 'Democracy in Germany' in *Germany in Transition*, p.4

# Index